# PRAY BIG
*for Your*
# CHILD

# PRAY BIG

*for Your*

# CHILD

The Power of Praying God's Promises
for Your Child's Life

## WILL DAVIS JR.

a division of Baker Publishing Group
Grand Rapids, Michigan

© 2009 by Will Davis Jr.

Published by Revell
a division of Baker Publishing Group
P.O. Box 6287, Grand Rapids, MI 49516-6287
www.revellbooks.com

Second printing, June 2009

Printed in the United States of America

Library of Congress Cataloging-in-Publication Data
Davis Will, 1962–
    Pray big for your child : the power of praying God's promises for your child's life / Will Davis, Jr.
        p.   cm.
    Includes bibliographical references.
    ISBN 978-0-8007-3246-2 (pbk.)
    1. Parents—Prayers and devotions. 2. Prayer—Biblical teaching.  I. Title.
BV4845.D38  2009
248.3'2085—dc22                                                    2008037948

Dedicated to Will Davis III, Emily Davis, and Sara Davis.
Each of you is an incredible answer to my prayers.

# CONTENTS

7

Contents

# ACKNOWLEDGMENTS

Thanks to . . .

Susie Davis—for inspiring, supporting, loving, and putting up with me. It's a pleasure to have a praying woman as the mother of my children.

Cathy Anderson, Linda Ayotte, Lizzie Benigno, Kathy Berke, Wendy Browning, Lisa Davis, Amy Duncan, Jeanne Marie Ellis, Dennis Fasetta, Nancy Fowler, Kerri Gerrie, Richard Hastings, Mike and Connie Helton, Lori Howe, Mike Kampen, Joni Kendrick, Nancy McDonald, Pam Moratta, Susan Murphy, Alan Nagel, Tonya Parrott, Pete Patterson, Lorri Payne, Cindy Present, Mike and Suzanne Schatzman, Jim Shearer, Eddy and Lynne Siroin, Andrea Smith, Les Stobbe, Lori Trenasty, Bill Walker, and Holly Wright—for sharing their inspiring prayers for their kids.

Sara and Chris Coltharp—for allowing me to participate in one of the coolest weddings ever.

Rebecca Davis—for standing up for your faith and for setting a great example for my girls.

Nancy, Mackenzie, and Eric Fowler—for being godly, inspiring people. I'm totally proud of you and love you all.

Mallory McGee—for inspiring me and for representing Christ so well.

Andy and Lynn Neillie—for being great friends and for modeling stewardship for Drew.

Lorri and Terry Payne—for being great friends, for supporting *Pray Big*, for having a godly family, and for contributing to this project.

Gary, Tracy, and Sydney Ramirez—for being great friends and for sharing your inspiring story.

Steve and Jillynn Shaver—for being a great example of praying parents.

Andrea and Curt Smith—for loving, serving, and supporting Susie and me.

Michael and Debbie Spell—for raising godly kids and for providing an inspiring teaching moment.

Rebecca Welch—for risking your life to save others.

David Guion—for being a great friend, a godly worship leader, and a mighty man of God.

Buddy and Melody White—for teaching me about generational momentum, and for changing yours.

Heather and Bobby Zugg—for raising godly boys, for being awesome Christian parents, and for taking time to help me on this project.

Kimmie Grimes, Shane Major, Hudson Baird, David Booth, and Hannah Parrott—for being great examples of kids with a mission.

Erika Dunham, Kelly Carter, Kate Stafford, and Megan Stafford—for being married to Jesus.

Joni Kendrick—for a decade of friendship, love, support, shared vision, and community. You are a great friend and you inspire me as a parent.

Wendy Browning—for great support and friendship, and for proofing the manuscript.

Terri Crow—for being a godly woman, a great mother, and a true servant. You are also the greatest proofreader of all time, period.

Tonya Parrott—for great support and for contributing to this manuscript.

Steve Shaver and Julie Washington—for leading ministries that prioritize and disciple kids. You both have taught me so much. I love serving with you.

Les Stobbe—for continued support and friendship.

The ever-growing ACF staff—for supporting me, for embracing the ACF vision, and for being a blast to work with. I love you all.

The ACF overseers and board—for inspiring and courageous leadership, and for encouraging me to write.

The people of Austin Christian Fellowship—for believing God and serving Jesus.

Vicki Crumpton—for great coaching, vision, and support. I love working with you. Thanks also for countless small talks about bikes, dogs, cats, trails, life, etc.

Suzie Cross Burden, Deonne Beron, Jessica Miles, Twila Bennett, Cheryl Van Andel, Karen Steele, Brooke Nolen, Debbie Deacon, Lonnie Hull DuPont, Claudia Marsh, and the incredible people at Revell and Baker Publishing Group—for everything you've done for the *Pray Big* books. You are all incredibly professional, godly, and a pleasure to work with.

# 1

## MARIAH'S MIRACLE
## (AND HER MOTHER'S PRAYER!)

MARIAH APPROACHED THE beginning of middle school as a happy, normal sixth grader. She was a good student, she would be attending her neighborhood school with her best girlfriends, and she was excited about the new adventure. But that all changed on the first day of school. Mariah basically experienced the equivalent of a panic attack. She started crying uncontrollably and inconsolably. Tragically, the scene was repeated almost every day of that school year. Her mother would drive her to school but was often unable to get Mariah out of the car. Other days, Mariah would make a brave attempt to face her school fears, only to spend most of the day in the counselor's office or crying at her desk. Her new adventure had turned into a nightmare.

During that time, Mariah's parents did everything they could to help her. They prayed for her and with her. She started seeing a professional Christian counselor, and her school counselor worked with her every day. She also started taking antidepressants.

The next year, as Mariah was about to enter seventh grade, she and her parents agreed that she would try a new school. It was a Christian school with a great reputation. Things started off smoothly enough for Mariah, but within just a few weeks, the panic attacks were back.

Mariah bottomed out in the late fall of her seventh grade year. Her mother, Kathleen, wrote, "It was the most gut-wrenching thing I've ever experienced, watching my child just try to slog through such misery. She was crying out to God. She was begging me for help. . . . It's so hard to convey how severe this was. I'm not talking about a bratty kid crying and refusing to get out of the car. I'm talking about true hysterics, rocking, making guttural sounds, etc."

Things were so bad that Kathleen and her husband drove Mariah to a local psychiatric hospital. They basically told Mariah that if she couldn't gain control of her fears, they would have to hospitalize her. It wasn't a threat; these Christian parents really didn't know how to help their daughter. The drugs, therapy, and prayers didn't seem to be working.

Mariah reluctantly agreed to give school another try. Kathleen remembers dropping her off and watching her frightened but determined seventh grader weeping as she disappeared through the school's doors. Kathleen wrote, "I got in my car and started sobbing, and then I prayed for her like I had done every other day. I was praying things like, 'O God, please help Mariah. Please, please, please. God, I know you hear her crying out to you. Why won't you help her? Please just help her put one foot in front of the other and make it through the day.'"

And then it happened. Kathleen had a breakthrough. As she sat in her car, praying for God to help Mariah survive the day, she clearly heard God say, "Is that really all you want from me?"

That's a really good question, isn't it? How many times have you gone to God in a moment of parental desperation and pleaded for mere survival? How often are we as Christian parents guilty of not asking for God's best provision but simply his bare minimum? How quickly do we forget while in our foxhole praying that Jesus promised abundant life to his children? Have you ever heard the Holy Spirit say, "Is that really all you want from me?" in response to your prayers?

Kathleen felt the gentle rebuke in the Spirit's question and decided to go for broke. She wrote, "So I just unleashed. I said, 'No, that's not all I want! I want Mariah to be great, not good! I want Mariah to be blessed! I want everyone who knows her to know that your hand is on her. I want everyone who meets my child to know that God has blessed her.'"[1]

And that's exactly what God did. Mariah didn't just survive that day, she actually enjoyed it. She was great, not just good. And she's been great just about every day since. Today Mariah is a happy teenager who is excelling in school. She has friends, dances on the drill team, makes good grades, and serves in her church. And she's completely off the antidepressants. Mariah is prevailing, not just surviving, because her mother obeyed the leading of God's Spirit and dared to ask for something big from God.

## Parenting by Prayer

It would be difficult to find a group of people in the Bible that God was more passionate about than children. Both testaments of the Bible speak to God's love for, concern for, and prioritization of kids. For a praying parent, the Bible is a treasure chest of promises that God is ready and willing to

> I pray that my kids will be leaders for Christ, that they will live lives that will make others curious about their faith. I pray that they will show strength, perseverance in trials, confidence, grace, and forgiveness. I pray that they will trust God in all circumstances and that they will see him at work in their lives and the lives of those around them.
>
> A praying mom

fulfill on behalf of a child. Even if you're new to the idea of praying for your child, it's never too late to learn. This book will show you how.

Prayer is the most effective tool a parent has. When teaching, discipline, and modeling fail, prayer succeeds. Prayer goes where a parent can't. It softens hard hearts, enlightens darkened minds, and guides lost souls. Prayer works.

As parents, we don't have to settle for having the kind of children that our society seems so determined to produce. As praying parents, we don't have to sit quietly by and watch while our sons and daughters are led astray by the allure of culture. Prayer is a parent's way of taking matters into *God's* hands.

So pray. Pray big, bold, biblical prayers for your child. God is ready to answer, and he doesn't want you to settle for less than his best or to compromise when you pray for your child. Pray big!

**Prayers That Work**

In the pages and chapters that follow, I want to show you how to offer biblical and highly effective prayers for your child. When you're finished with this book, I believe you'll feel much more confident about how you pray for your kid and better equipped to cover him or her with biblical promises in just about every stage and situation in life.

So what do you say? Are you ready to learn how to raise your child one prayer at a time? If so, then keep reading.

**Verses to Pray for Your Child**

To help get you started praying for your child, and to give you a taste of what's to come, here are three very powerful biblical promises you can start praying right now.

- Numbers 6:24–26: *Lord, please bless and keep my child; make your face shine upon her and be gracious to her; turn your face toward her and give her peace.*
- Ephesians 1:3: *Jesus, thank you for already giving my child every spiritual blessing that you possess. Please help him to realize how blessed he is and to live the spiritually rich life that you gave him through your death.*
- 1 Timothy 6:12: *Lord God, help my children to fight the good fight of the faith. May they take hold of the eternal life to which they were called when they made their good confession in the presence of many witnesses.*

# PART 1

# PRINCIPLES
# OF PINPOINT PRAYING

This, then, is how you should pray.

Matthew 6:9

# 2

# Pinpoint Praying versus No-Point Praying

How many times have you settled for the "Lord, just help my child to survive" kind of praying that Kathleen wrote about in the last chapter? How often have you mumbled some weak, pathetic prayer in hopes that God would help you or your child just to get by? Have you ever thought about that? Have you ever thought about how ridiculously low we set the bar when it comes to praying for our kids? One would think that we were dealing with the little man behind the curtain who pretends to be the great wizard of Oz, instead of with the holy and creating God of the universe. Why do we frequently ask so little of God when it comes to our kids?

Perhaps you've prayed one of the following prayers:

- God, please keep Sally from getting pregnant.
- God, help David not to become an alcoholic like his father.

- God, please help Jake to pass math.
- God, please keep Tommy from getting hurt in football.
- God, please help Sharon to be nice to her friends at school.
- God, please help Timmy not to wet his pants today.
- God, help me and Joe not to argue today about his chores.

While there's nothing really wrong with this type of praying, it doesn't ask or require much of God. Do you hear the "Lord, just help us to get by" mind-set of those prayers? It's as if the parent is approaching a God who is irritated and worn-out by the parent's constant pestering—as if God might react as we parents do when we're tired and irritable. But God is not an irritable parent. He never grows weary of our requests to him. And while there is nothing wrong with praying for little things, we should not settle for small answers when God has promised that all of his power is available to us when we ask. And when it comes to our kids—really, they're *his* kids—we shouldn't skimp. We need to pray with focus and not toss up weak and wimpy petitions to our holy God.

I'm talking about the difference between what I call pinpoint praying and no-point praying. We can't afford to waste our time by praying no-point prayers for our kids. No-point prayers resemble the "God be with Bill," "God bless Sue" kind of praying that doesn't ask anything of God. More specifically, no-point praying is:

- *Too broad*—No-point praying asks God to cure world hunger or save all the people on earth. Broad prayers sound good on the surface but rarely have any real courage or passion behind them.

22

- *Too vague*—This is the essence of the "God bless Joe" kinds of prayers. They're fuzzy and have no real meaning. They don't really ask anything tangible of God.
- *Too safe*—No-point prayers don't require any faith. There's no risk at all in praying them, because nothing that requires God to act is ever asked of him.

No-point prayers are completely inadequate when it comes to our children. They're too broad, vague, and faithless to be offered as real prayers for our kids. You and I know our children deserve better. God also commanded us to pray better than that. What he expects of us is pinpoint praying.

Pinpoint prayers, as opposed to no-point prayers, have clear purpose, direction, and focus. They're the kind of prayers that honor God the most, and they're the kind that you and I want to be praying for our children. Pinpoint prayers are:

- *Biblical*—Pinpoint prayers are deeply rooted in God's Word. They have authority because they flow right out of what God has already told us he is willing to do. There's no guesswork in pinpoint praying. As a parent, you just take the world's greatest prayer script (the Bible) and use it as your guide for what and how you pray for your kids. (I'll show you how to do this in the next chapter.)
- *Specific*—There's nothing vague about pinpoint prayers. They're typically short, direct, and to the point. Consider Jesus's petitions in the Lord's Prayer. His requests for God's name to be glorified and for God's provision, protection, and forgiveness are all very specific and focused. There's nothing broad or uncertain about them. Pinpoint praying requires you to think through what you want God to do, build the case for it biblically, and then say it in the most precise and deliberate way possible to God. No flowery language, no King James English, and

23

no long or theologically loaded phrases are required with pinpoint prayers. Part of their power lies in their directness.

- *Bold*—Pinpoint prayers don't mess around. They don't dance around an issue, hoping that God will get the hint and come through with a miracle without us really having to ask for one. Pinpoint prayers walk right up to God's throne and plead for his best, for his kingdom, and for his favor in our lives and the lives of our children. This is not weak-willed praying. This is grabbing hold of God in prayer and wrestling with him until he comes through for your kids (see Gen. 32:24–30). Can you think of any area where boldness, courage, and faith are more appropriate than in prayers for your kids?

Prayer is the most significant form of communication that humans, specifically parents, can engage in. When a Christian talks to God, all the power of heaven is at play, and cultures, nations, and history lay in the balance. For parents, talking to our kids is critical; talking to God about them is even more so.

## Taking a Cue from Kids

Have you ever listened to children recite their wish lists while sitting on Santa's lap at the mall? Don't you love their faith, their innocence? "I want a new house, a horse for my sister, and my grandma to feel better. And I want to meet the president and go on a trip to Disney World." Granted, there's something a bit self-centered about most of those wishes, but that's not unusual for a child. Jesus still pointed to children as great examples of kingdom citizens, and it wasn't because of their self-focus. I believe it was because of their faith.

Children have no problem asking for big things. They don't worry about where stuff comes from or how parents or Santa will get it in the house or down the chimney. They don't fret over where they'll put a horse or if they can afford the trip to Disney World. They just ask, and then they believe. And when they ask, they typically ask big. Jesus pointed to children as great examples for adult believers because their hearts are innocent and naive enough to still believe huge things of God.

> The prayer that I pray for our children and grandchildren is, "Lord, protect their hearts for yourself!"
>
> A praying father and grandfather

Pray for such a heart. Pray for the simple, naive faith of a child. Ask God to equip you to believe and expect big things of him in prayer. Ask God to show you how to pray big, hairy, audacious prayers for your child.

## A Verse to Pray for Your Child

Psalm 19:13: *Father, please keep my child from willful sins; may they not rule over her. Help her to be blameless, innocent of great transgression.*

# 3

# BIG, HAIRY, AUDACIOUS PRAYERS FOR YOUR CHILD

I N MY BOOK *Pray Big*,[1] I wrote about the concept of Big, Hairy, Audacious Prayers (BHAPs), a concept inspired by Jim Collins's discussion of Big, Hairy, Audacious Goals (BHAGs) in his bestselling book *Built to Last*. Readers seemed to love the concept of BHAPs but often didn't know how to apply them to specific areas of their lives. While I was researching this book, one mother wrote to me, "What would be helpful? Well, I know what I want for my kids, but I know that their heavenly Father wants even more for them. So I guess that I would like to be inspired to pray big for my kids. I can't really even think of what a BHAP, in line with God's will, would be for my kids. Does that make sense?"

It makes complete sense. None of us wants to be guilty of under-praying for our children, but neither do we want to presume on God with our huge requests. How do we know when we're on target with our BHAPs? Here are a few reminders.

## Characteristics of BHAPs

### BHAPs Are God-Centered

At the heart of every good BHAP is a desire to honor and exalt God. God didn't give us the ability to seek big things from him for our own benefit or self-promotion. He does want to give us huge answers to our prayers for ourselves, our families, and our areas of concern, but he wants to do so for his honor and glory, not ours. Psalm 115:1 is a great guide when praying our BHAPs: "Not to us, O LORD, not to us but to your name be the glory, because of your love and faithfulness." Remember the first petition of the Lord's Prayer: "Lord, let your name be hallowed! Let your name be exalted!" (see Matt. 6:9).

When praying for your child, don't seek great things for him so you can live vicariously through him or look smart as a parent. If your motive in prayer is ever about promoting you, your family, your name, or your agenda, then your BHAP ceases to be effective. Before you bring your big, hairy, audacious requests for yourself or your child before God, make sure that you've stripped away all the ego and self-gratification from them. God loves to honor prayers that ultimately seek his honor and glory.

### BHAPs Are Based on Vision and Calling

We need to pray big, hairy, audacious prayers for our kids because God has called us to and has given us a vision of what he wants to do in our children. Great BHAPs don't originate in the heart of a parent; they originate in the heart of God. He knows far better than we do what our kids need and what's best for them.

There's no pretension or bravado in a BHAP. Your prayer for your kid to win a Heisman trophy or be a top runway model can just as easily be based on pride and presumption than a genuine desire for God to be honored in your child. Big, hairy, audacious prayers for your child, if not Spirit-led, usually end up being more ego-driven, not God-driven. The best BHAPs are those given to us by God for our children. Let God direct your praying for your child. Seek a vision from him for your child's future, and then pray that vision. God's vision and plans for your child will always be better and brighter than yours.

### BHAPs Are Biblical

Like the pinpoint prayers we mentioned above, BHAPs never contradict God's Word. Without question, the best litmus test for the purity of a BHAP is the Bible.

Rogue BHAPs won't pass the sniff test of Scripture. I've often been guilty of praying for my kids to get the best of an enemy, to beat a rival, or to outshine a classmate, only to be reminded that my prayers weren't really based on a biblical mind-set. My prayers for my child to excel should never be at the expense or embarrassment of another person. My prayer years ago for my son to be prepared to "beat the daylights" out of a school bully may have been big and hairy, but it was difficult to justify with Scripture.

Before you take your BHAPs to God, make sure they're biblical. Ask yourself, *Would Jesus pray for this?* If not, then you need to rethink what you're asking.

### BHAPs Can't Be Manipulated

We love to help God. Somehow we've gotten the idea that God actually needs our assistance. For instance, I might pray that my daughter gets into a really great college, and then I call the school's president to make sure that her application gets placed on the top of the admissions pile. That's helping God.

But what do you do when you can't manipulate the outcome? What do you do when your needs far exceed any ability you have to fulfill them? That's where big, hairy, audacious praying kicks in, and that's where God wants you to live as a Christ-follower.

> I pray that my children will see and hear Christ in me, that I will be a light that will forever leave an imprint on their hearts, and that they will desire to know Christ better because of what they see in me.
>
> A praying mom

God doesn't want you settling for the best you can do. He doesn't want you to only ask things for your child that you can manage or control. God wants you praying in a way that requires his divine participation. Anything less shortchanges God and misses the point of prayer.

When Kathleen prayed for Mariah to prevail at school, she asked for something to affect the outcome that was well beyond her capacities. She needed a miracle. BHAPs aren't always born out of such dire circumstances, but they do have the same sense of dependency on God.

Don't always pray something for your child that you can do yourself. What's the point? If that's all you ever pray for, then you are asking your kid to settle for the best that *you* can do for him. When it comes to your kid, that's not good enough! Pray for things that only God can do. Then your child will get God's best, not yours.

## Discovering Your Child's BHAPs

There's no formula for discovering how to pray big for your child. In fact, it's probably much more of a natural process than you think. If you're a praying person, then it's quite likely that God is already showing you what and how to pray for your kid. But if you're not certain, ask him.

I suggested above that BHAPs flow out of a God-given calling and vision. If you're not sure whether or not you're on target with your prayers for your kid, ask God to guide you in the process. Use Jeremiah 29:11 as your guide: "Lord, I know you have amazing plans for my child, plans that I can't even begin to fathom. I know that you have a future and a hope for her. Would you please show me how to pray according to your will and your Word for my child? Would you please show me how to pray big for her?" God loves that kind of praying. Your humility and willingness to submit to his plan for your child is all the invitation he needs to show you what great and mighty things you can pray for her.

Once you've asked God to show you how to pray for your child, pause and take a survey of the passions and areas of concern you have for her. What do you hope for her? In what ways is she weak and subject to temptation? What particular gifts and skills has God given her? What unique physical, emotional, or mental challenges does she face? What types of relational and emotional issues or addictive tendencies has she inherited from you, your spouse, or your extended family that you want God to heal? If you could snap your fingers and guarantee blessing and success in just one area of your child's life, what would it be?

Make a list of the issues you feel most passionate about for your child, and then start searching the Bible for promises that speak to those issues. The Bible is your BHAP treasure chest. It's loaded with countless promises that speak of God's desire to heal, protect, anoint, grow, prosper, and bless his children. Use it as your guide when praying for your child.

You don't necessarily need to do a literal Bible study or Bible search for verses to pray for your child. Just keep your eyes and heart open for God to speak to you about your child whenever you read his Word. For instance, I was reading my Bible recently when I read Psalm 119:112: "My heart is set on keeping your decrees to the very end." I've read those words on dozens, if not hundreds, of occasions, but for some reason I felt led that day to pray them for my children. I wrote each of their initials next to the verse and prayed something like, *Dear God, make these words true for Will, Emily, and Sara. I pray that they would each set their heart on your Word and determine to keep it no matter what. Make them strong, determined, faithful Christ-followers every day of their lives. Help them never to stray from you.*

In today's world, where a large majority of kids raised in church decide to quit attending and even stop believing during their college and postcollege years,[2] that's a big, hairy, audacious prayer. Now, whenever I read Psalm 119:112 in my Bible, I'm reminded to pray that BHAP for my kids.

You can do the same. Let the Bible speak to you about your child and how to pray for her. As you do, the Holy Spirit will lead you to a rich storehouse of promises that God wants you to pray for your kid—just so he can answer.

Finally, pray! After you've sought God for his guidance, after you've surveyed and indexed your passions for your child, and as you consistently read God's Word and discover beautiful pinpoint promises—pray. God has promised to do amazing things for your child. Pray until he does.

In Isaiah 62:6–7, Isaiah promised to never be silent and to "give him [God] no rest" until he kept his promises regarding Jerusalem. If you read the subsequent verses, you'll find that God was pleased with, not put off by, Isaiah's boldness (see Isa. 62:8–12). We should be as bold and persistent. You would be hard-pressed to find a more biblical, God-honoring topic for profound and prolonged intercession than the spiritual well-being of children. So don't be timid. Place your child's emotional, spiritual, and physical needs at the top of your prayer list, and then present their needs to God every day for the rest of your life. As you pray these powerful pinpoint prayers and BHAPs for your child, you'll see God move consistently and graciously on her behalf.

## A Verse to Pray for Your Child

Isaiah 50:4: *Sovereign Lord, please give my child an instructed tongue, so that she will know the words that sustain the weary.*

# PART 2

# PINPOINT PRAYERS
# FOR YOUR CHILD

And he took the children in his arms, put his hands on them
and blessed them.

Mark 10:16

# 4

# Laying a Good Foundation

## Pinpoint Prayers Every Parent Needs to Pray

I N 586 BC Nebuchadnezzar, king of the powerful Babylonian Empire, captured Jerusalem, killed most of the adults in the city, and deported many of the young people over six hundred miles back to Babylon. He immediately began an indoctrination program for the most promising of the Hebrew youths. They were tutored in Babylonian literature, social customs, politics, mythology, and religion. Nebuchadnezzar's goal was clear: erase all traces of the Hebrew culture in these youths and raise them to be great citizens of Babylon. The king even went so far as to rename the youths with proper Babylonian names.

Daniel, the main character of the Old Testament book that bears his name, was one of these deported young men. When he and his friends left Jerusalem, they probably did so as orphans. If they were going to keep the lamp of their Hebrew culture and faith burning brightly, they were going to have to do it without the help and support of their parents.

How would your kids do in that situation? Do they have enough spiritual training and discipline to withstand the kind of shock and tests that Daniel faced? Have you shown them how to love and serve God even in difficult circumstances?

The king ordered that Daniel and some of his friends be given a special diet of wine and food from his royal table. He no doubt looked disparagingly on the foolish food prohibitions and customs taught in the Hebrew Scriptures. Nebuchadnezzar wanted these boys fattened up for his service and for the voluptuous life of Babylonian culture. But Daniel knew better. He had been taught that God's law wasn't to be broken and that great benefit and favor could be found in keeping it, even in the face of repercussions. So Daniel and his three friends proposed a test to their caretaker: "Please test your servants for ten days: Give us nothing but vegetables to eat and water to drink. Then compare our appearance with that of the young men who eat the royal food, and treat your servants in accordance with what you see" (Dan. 1:12–13).

I love the courage and faith in God that Daniel showed. He really believed that if he remained faithful, God would honor his obedience. You know what? He was right: "At the end of the ten days they looked healthier and better nourished than any of the young men who ate the royal food" (v. 15). Not only did God honor Daniel's decision not to compromise his diet, but he also exalted Daniel and his friends before the king: "In every matter of wisdom and understanding about which the king questioned them, he found them ten times better than all the magicians and enchanters in his whole kingdom" (v. 20).

Daniel's leadership role and favor in Babylon ended up extending into the reigns of the next two monarchs after Nebuchadnezzar. There's no doubt that if Daniel had compromised his faith and obedience, he not only wouldn't have excelled in Babylon, but we also wouldn't be reading about him 2,600 years later.

What's the point? Daniel excelled in Babylon by adhering to God's Word. If you want your kids to excel in Babylon (and trust me, they do live in Babylon), then they must do the same. Spiritual favor isn't found by becoming like the Babylonians; it's found in being faithful to God. Daniel had the spiritual training and foundation to remain true to his faith even in the midst of overwhelming spiritual and cultural opposition, and he did so while still in his teens.

Kids don't come by that sort of spiritual wisdom and tenacity by default. It has to be taught, modeled, and, most of all, prayed into them. As you think about your children's lives, you know that there are some foundational things that you want for them, some basic principles that you want to be true for them every day. Why not turn those foundational desires into foundational pinpoint prayers?

## How Firm a Foundation

In this chapter, let's learn how to pray for those most important realities and needs in our kids' lives. Let's learn how to lay a great foundation for their lives through prayer. Regardless of your child's age, you'll find the pinpoint prayers in this chapter relevant, helpful, encouraging, and effective.

### Pray that your child will awaken to the reality of God.

Belief in God is natural. We are wired from birth to know him. For a child to grow up not believing in God, some serious suppressing of truth has to occur. Thus, you can be sure that when you create an environment that is conducive to your child discovering God, he or she will.

Ecclesiastes 3:11 tells us that God placed eternity into the hearts of all people. From our births, we are designed to seek out that which is eternal; we are designed to seek after God. Your child has a built-in spiritual homing device, and perhaps he is now old enough to begin to feel its pull. Pray that your child will begin to recognize the tug of God on his heart. Pray that he will become aware of the spiritual realities around him. Pray that he will believe what his heart is telling him and will discover and embrace the reality of God.

Pray Psalm 71:5 for your child: *Sovereign Lord, I pray that you will be my child's hope and his confidence all the days of his life.*

### Pray that your child will have a healthy fear of God.

The fear of the Lord is almost extinct in today's Christianity. It's a misunderstood concept, often mistaken for being afraid of the God who can't wait to throw lightning bolts at cowering sinners. But that's not what biblical fear is. To fear God is to have a healthy respect for him, but it's more than just respect. It's to revere him, to know that while he is good, he is also infinite, holy, and all-powerful. To fear God is to approach him with love and awe.

God promises to honor those who fear him. Consider these promises:

> The LORD confides in those who fear him; he makes his covenant known to them.
>
> Psalm 25:14

> He who fears the LORD has a secure fortress, and for his children it will be a refuge. The fear of the LORD is a fountain of life, turning a man from the snares of death.
>
> Proverbs 14:26–27

The fear of the LORD leads t
untouched by trouble.

Your child is growing up
and discredits the nature a
child to be different. Yo
fear God rather than pe
pleasing others. Your child is nev
start learning about the importance of fearing

Pray that your child will develop a healthy and appropria.
fear of the Lord. Pray Psalm 2:11 for her: *Lord God, I pray
that my child will serve you with a holy fear and rejoice before
you with trembling.*

### Pray that your child will develop a godly character.

I had a high school football coach who was fond of saying,
"Character is what you do when no one is looking at you."
Even as a young, immature high school kid, I knew what he
meant. Our character, who we really are at our core, is best
revealed by what we do and how we act when we're alone.
The ancient Greek philosophers put it this way: "Character
is best revealed in the dark."

We certainly have no shortage of "characters" in the spot-
light of today's culture. What we do seem to be lacking, however, is a ready supply of character. Being a character and
having it are not the same. You want your child to grow up
with an unshakable inner core—a clear knowledge of who he
or she is in Christ and the personal grit not to compromise
it. That's character.

In Hebrews 1:3, the writer described Jesus as "the radiance
of God's glory and the exact representation of his being."
The word used for "exact representation" is the Greek word

r English word *character* comes from it. *Ka-* from a root word that means "to cut" or "to s the idea of an artist engraving an image in metal that is an exact replica of the original. That's what ter is: a deeply embedded engraving in the soul of a on that tells him who he is (and isn't).

Character is formed in the early years of a child's life. Those early developmental years are the best time for a child to begin to learn about the principles of right and wrong and to develop the personal courage to always do what's right even when it's hard. Thus, we need to start praying for our child's character from the moment she is born.

Pray that your child's soul will be engraved with the same heart, attitude, courage, and wisdom as Jesus. Pray Hebrews 1:3 for your child: *Father, I pray that my child will develop the character of Christ. Let her be an exact representation of Jesus's heart and attitudes.*

### Pray that your child will love obedience.

I don't know many people, especially kids, who think of the word *obey* in a positive sense. The word just seems to reek of forced compliance and lost freedoms. But as a growing Christ-follower and a parent, you know that obedience is that place where safety, joy, and blessing most frequently meet. You want your child to obey not just you but God as well.

Your home is the best classroom for teaching the benefits of obedience. As your child learns the advantages and reasons for obeying you, he'll also begin to learn about the spiritual benefits of obeying God. Pray that your child will learn the power and blessing of obedience. Pray that he will learn to obey instantly. Pray that he won't negotiate or stall in his obedience to God.

In Deuteronomy 28, God went to great lengths to communicate through Moses to his people the blessings of obedience and the curses of disobedience. In verse 1, he promised that if they obeyed him, he would set them high over all the nations of the earth. (For one of the best and clearest descriptions in the Bible of the fruits of obedience and the curses of disobedience, read all of Deuteronomy 28.) In John 12:26, Jesus made a similar statement when he promised that his Father would honor those who served him. In both verses, you hear God saying, "I love to honor obedience!"

Pray that your child will know that. Pray that he'll understand the immediate benefits of following, serving, and obeying Christ, and the immediate pain that comes with disobedience. Pray that he'll see obedience and compliance to God's Word as a blessing and not a chore, as a privilege and not a burden. Pray that he will always practice obedience no matter how difficult or costly. Then ask God to honor your child as he obeys him. Pray that God will be pleased with him and that he'll be quick to promote him when he is faithful.

My college-age son recently made a difficult personal decision. He made the tough choice to defer to others and to yield in a situation where he could have clearly asserted his rights and looked out for himself. No one would have blamed him for making the decision that would have been best for him. But my son couldn't. He really felt God leading him to defer and not exert his rights and, by doing so, to trust and obey God. The results of my son's decision have had profound, long-term effects in his life. His obedience has not been easy. But he's starting to see the fruit of his decision. He told me recently, "This is hard, but I sleep better at night knowing that I did what God wanted me to do."

I'm so proud of him for making that call. I'm proud of him for choosing obedience over comfort and over any sense of entitlement. And, of course, his mother and I are praying that God will greatly honor our son's obedience.

Pray the same for your child. Pray Psalm 40:8 for him: *Father, help my child to desire to do your will; place your law within his heart.*

### Pray that God's favor will rest on your child.

The Hebrew concept of favor appears frequently in the Old Testament. A favored person received goodwill and acceptance from others and often experienced the blessings that accompanied such goodwill. God's favor was especially important in the lives of many Old Testament heroes. Abel, Cain's brother and Adam and Eve's son, was favored by God when he offered his sacrifice in worship. Noah and Lot were both spared disaster because God favored them. Jacob's youngest son, Joseph, knew God's favor from an early age, and it protected him even after he was sold into slavery and thrown into prison in Egypt. Esther was favored by God and granted acceptance in the eyes of her king. In many cases, the favor of God on people's lives carried far beyond their own personal blessing. It often meant that God blessed their families and even their nation.

Hannah, Samuel's mother, prayed for a child even when she couldn't bear children. She promised to dedicate her baby to God if he would grant her the favor of motherhood. A year later, God gave her a special baby boy. The Bible notes that young Samuel "continued to grow in stature and *in favor* with the LORD and with men" (1 Sam. 2:26, emphasis added). Interestingly, the writer Luke uses a similar phrase to describe the early development of the Lord Jesus (see Luke 2:52).

Consider the example of Mary, the young mother of Jesus. We know very little about her childhood. She was a faithful Hebrew and probably relatively poor. We also know that she was chosen by God for a tremendous and difficult task. When the angel Gabriel spoke with her, he identified her as one who was "highly favored" by God (Luke 1:28). What did Gabriel mean by that? What does it mean to be highly favored?

The Greek word that Luke used for *favored* comes from the root word for *grace*. Gabriel identified Mary as one who had quite literally been highly graced by God. *Grace*, simply stated, is the merciful and benevolent act of God on behalf of an undeserving party. To be graced or favored by God is to receive undue esteem, honor, or blessing from him. Grace is never solicited or merited by the beneficiary. It is given out of the magnificent love of God's heart and has nothing to do with the deserving status of the recipient.

I find the implications of Luke's wording to be quite refreshing. Rather than being a unique or almost divine type of person, Mary was an ordinary young teen. I have no doubts that Mary was godly and that she was a faithful, devout Hebrew youth. But as such, Mary was like countless other young Hebrew women who really loved and honored their God. Thus, God's selection of Mary for the awesome assignment of bearing the Lord Jesus was based on his favor and goodness to her, not on any special or deserving status she exhibited. And it is that exact favor and goodness from God that we need to seek on behalf of our children.

Pray for your child to be favored by God. Ask that God's favor would rest on her. Psalm 30:5 promises that God's favor lasts a lifetime. Pray every day that your child would know God's favor all of her life. Pray that because of God's favor, your child would be a blessing to others.

Pray Psalm 90:17 for your child: *Lord God, may your favor rest upon my child; establish the work of her hands for her—yes, establish the work of her hands.*

## Pray that your child will grow up knowing the Scriptures.

In Paul's second letter to his young disciple, Timothy, he commented on the boy's strong spiritual heritage. Even though his father was an unbeliever, Timothy had a mother and grandmother who were great women of faith. It seems that they raised young Timothy to know and love God, even from his earliest childhood days. Paul urged Timothy to "continue in what you have learned and have become convinced of, because you know those from whom you learned it, and how from infancy you have known the holy Scriptures, which are able to make you wise for salvation through faith in Christ Jesus" (2 Tim. 3:14–15).

Paul believed that Timothy's strong faith could be traced back to the earliest days of his life. He believed that Timothy had been aware of the teachings of Scripture "from infancy."

> We pray that our children would embrace the Word of God and live it on a daily basis. We pray that they would fall in love with God, hate sin, and run as far away from sin as possible.
>
> A praying husband and wife

But what did Paul mean? What does it mean to know the Scriptures from infancy? Simply stated, it means that Timothy grew up hearing God's Word. It means that his mother and grandmother were instructing him in the ways of God and quoting God's Word to him, even before he was old enough to understand what they were saying. It means that he grew up against the backdrop of the Holy Scriptures.

Isn't that a beautiful picture? Pray that it would be true for your child. Pray that he will grow up knowing and loving the Bible and that the truth of God would be a natural part of his life. Pray Psalm 22:10 for him: *Lord, may my child be able to say: "From birth I was cast upon you; from my mother's womb you have been my God."*

### Pray that your child will recognize God's voice.

The example of young Samuel in 1 Samuel 3:1–10 tells us that hearing and then recognizing God's voice is an acquired skill. Even though he was being raised and trained by a prophet in a very God-centered environment, Samuel didn't immediately recognize God's voice. It took him a while to figure out what God's voice sounded like.

God is a great communicator and wants us to hear him. However, like young Samuel, we have to develop our spiritual listening skills. And there's no better time to start learning to hear God than when we're young.

Start praying that your child will begin to learn to discern God's voice. An early school-aged child isn't too young to start learning to listen to God. Jesus repeatedly emphasized that those who understood his kingdom would have the heart, the faith, and the attitude of a child.

Children can hear God. We need to raise them to *expect* to hear him. Pray that your child, like Samuel, will learn at an early age to hear God's voice. Pray John 10:27 for her: *Lord Jesus, I pray that my child will listen to your voice and that she will follow you.*

### Pray that your child will marry a godly person.

Not long after I found out that Susie was expecting our first child, I started praying for his spouse. It wasn't a moment too soon. Next to the decision to follow Christ, your child's choice of a mate will probably be the most important and impacting life decision he or she will make. As a pastor, I've watched countless young Christ-followers sabotage their own spiritual futures by making poor marriage choices. Even if your child is still young, it won't be too long before he or she begins having serious romantic feelings toward others. He or she will start to have crushes, "go steady," "go out," and eventually date people. Any one of those people is a potential spouse. So if you haven't already started praying for your child's spouse, start now!

Your child's future mate is out in the world right now, making life choices and moral choices, establishing family and faith values, and engaging in relationships. Everything he or she does will affect his or her relationship with your child. It's not at all too early to start praying for your child's spouse.

I want to be able to look at the young woman who will marry my son and the young men who will marry my daughters, and tell them that I have been praying for them since they were children. And I want my kids to have the wisdom and discernment to marry godly people.

Here are some great pinpoint prayers to pray for your child's future marriage:

- Pray that your child's spouse will love Jesus more than he or she loves your child.
- Pray that your child will date godly people who love Christ.
- Pray that your child's relationships will stay sexually pure.
- Pray for the families—the parents and siblings—of your child's spouse. Pray that your child's future spouse will grow up in a home that honors and serves Jesus.
- Pray that your child will be willing and content to remain single until God brings him or her an equally godly spouse.

Pray Genesis 24:3–4 for your child: *Holy Father, please bring my child a godly spouse from among your people.*

## A Verse to Pray for Your Child

Luke 2:40: *Father, I pray that my child will grow and become strong, that he will be filled with wisdom, and that the grace of God will rest upon him.*

# 5

# From the Rising
# of the Sun

Pinpoint Prayers for Your Child's Daily Life

I N CONVERSATIONS WITH Christian moms, I have heard that they struggle with exactly *what* to pray for their kids. They want their kids to be accepted and feel good about themselves, but they don't feel comfortable praying, 'Let Julie be popular,' or, 'Let John make a touchdown.' I even struggle with that one. For instance, I want our kids to really like football (or other sports) and to do well. So do I pray for Tyler to make touchdowns? How silly." So wrote Joni, a praying mom.

Can you relate to Joni's tension? Is it silly to pray for your kid to hit home runs in Little League or to ace the SAT? Is it wrong to pray that your daughter will get the lead in the school play or that your son will have the most popular teacher for his third grade year?

God is the perfect parent. Because of that, things that matter to you and your child also matter to him. He wants to be involved in every detail of your lives, even those that seem mundane. So, if it's important to you for your kid not to be embarrassed at his first school dance because he has two left feet, God cares about that. If your heart is breaking for your daughter who feels rejected by her friends, then God hurts with you and wants to comfort both you and your daughter.

My advice to parents who ask if it's okay to pray about their kid's first day of kindergarten, spelling bee, math quiz, basketball tournament, first date, or cheerleader tryout is always, "Go for it; pray your heart out. God wants you to talk to him about everything, not just the 'big' things." From the time your child wakes up in the morning to the moment she lays her head down at night, exhausted from a full day, she needs prayer!

## Covering the Bases

In appendix 2, I offer you twelve specific prayer prompters to keep you praying for your child throughout the day. In the rest of this chapter, I want us to learn how to pray for those important matters that are part of our kids' daily lives.

### Pray that your child will be protected.

My girls love horses. My wife, Susie, rode as a young girl, and she quickly passed on her love for horses and riding to our two daughters. They've spent many a Saturday and weekday after school at our local barn.

Riding is a great sport. It teaches our girls discipline, hard work, and how to be patient and careful with strong, beautiful animals. Riding and jumping is an incredibly athletic and demanding sport. It can also be very dangerous.

When my youngest daughter, Sara, was only nine, she was training on a beautiful paint filly named Tiger Lilly. The two were working their way through a series of two-and-a-half-foot jumps in a large, sandy training ring. Coming out of one of the jumps, Tiger Lilly stumbled and went down on one knee. Sara tried to adjust her weight to stay atop the filly, but as the horse regained her balance, Sara's weight shifted again, and she went flying right over the head of the horse. All of this happened in a matter of a second or two, as Tiger Lilly was running in a full canter.

Susie was sitting on the side of the ring with some other moms. She could only watch in horror as our daughter disappeared under the horse in a terrifying mix of sand, hooves, and little girl. When the dust settled, Tiger Lilly was standing off to one side, and Sara lay motionless in a heap right where she had fallen. When Susie reached Sara, she was unresponsive. Her face was covered with sand, her helmet was broken, and she was bleeding on her forehead. It was a horrible sight. Susie began yelling, trying to elicit some type of response from Sara. As she moved to pick her up, Sara's eyelids opened, and her eyes rolled back in her head. Then she slowly focused in on her mother. After just a few minutes, Sara was able to answer questions such as, "What is your name?" "How old are you?" and "What day is this?" She was going to be okay.

Sara escaped her close call with a trip to the emergency room, a cut forehead, a concussion, and head-to-toe bruises. We credit a horse that somehow managed to avoid stepping on Sara and lots of closely watching and alert angels for her good fortune. Things could have been much worse. The whole incident reminded me of how dangerous riding can be and how I always need to be praying for my children's protection.

As your child grows older, she's going to become more independent and begin trying new things. Every day she's going to have ample opportunities to learn, grow, and become more mature. She's supposed to—that's part of growing up. It's also your cue to increase your prayers for her spiritual, emotional, and physical protection.

Skinned knees and hurt feelings are going to happen. Your child is going to take some tumbles in her everyday life—physically and emotionally. That's why you need to be praying for her protection. You want your child to walk through only the pain and suffering that God deems necessary and appropriate for her sanctification and character development. You want God to protect her from making unwise choices and from the pain that others can bring into her life. You want your child to grow through pain, not just suffer in it.

Pray for her protection. Pray that God will watch over her and keep her safe. Pray for protection from other people, from dangerous or bad circumstances, from temptation, and from Satan. Pray that God will allow only the pain that will grow your child more into the image of Jesus. Pray Psalm 32:7 for your child: *Father, be my child's hiding place; protect her from trouble and surround her with songs of deliverance.*

### Pray that your child will love learning.

I have a good friend who is an incredibly gifted worship leader. His sensitivity to the Holy Spirit helps him guide congregations through powerful and life-changing encounters with God through worship. My friend is also a very skilled musician. He works hard at sharpening and improving his musical skills. I once asked him about the balance between the Holy Spirit's anointing and talent: was one more important than the other? His answer surprised me. Even though his worship leading is anointed, he seemed to really emphasize the importance of hard work and talent. He said, "I want to be an incredibly sharp tool in the Spirit's hands. The better I am musically, the more I have to offer the Spirit for his work. I don't want to limit what the Spirit can do through me because of my lack of skill."

What my friend believes about musical talent is equally true about learning. We live in one of the most highly educated cultures in history. The opportunities for learning that we and our children have are limitless. We need to be good stewards of the opportunities God affords us. But beyond that, we need to learn and grow, because doing so makes us sharper, more effective tools in God's hands.

Pray that your child will love learning. Pray that he will take full advantage of the opportunities given him to go to school, to study, and to gain new experiences. Pray that your child will be a finely tuned instrument in God's hands.

Consider again the example of Daniel. When he and his friends were deported to Babylon, one of the reasons they were chosen was because of their high aptitude for learning. The Bible states that the king specifically asked for "young men without any physical defect, handsome, showing aptitude for every kind of learning, well informed, quick to understand, and qualified to serve in the king's palace" (Dan. 1:4). Nebuchadnezzar knew the importance of good learning and education in leadership. That's why he looked for young men who showed such great potential. Daniel's discipline for learning was another reason that he rose to such a high position of prominence in Babylon. Not only was he a young man of great faith, but he also had a great mind. He was a sharp, double-edged sword in God's hands, and God used him mightily.

The children we are raising in our homes today are the future leaders of our cities, our churches, and our nation. We obviously need to pray for their faith and passion for

God. We want them to be sold-out to his cause. But we also need to encourage them to learn. We want them to take full advantage of the chances they have to grow and expand their minds. We want them to be hungry for knowledge and curious about the world they live in. We want them to know that all truth belongs to God—spiritual truth, academic truth, and scientific truth—and not to be afraid of or intimidated by what they may read in a textbook or learn in the classroom.

Pray Daniel 1:4 for your child. Pray that he will develop an aptitude for every kind of learning, be well informed, be quick to understand, and be qualified to serve in the palace of the King of Kings. Pray that he will develop good study habits and will thrive in a classroom setting.

Proverbs 22:29 says, "Do you see a man skilled in his work? He will serve before kings; he will not serve before obscure men." Pray that for your child. Pray that because of his skills and aptitude, he will serve before leaders and people of influence. And pray Proverbs 1:5 for him: *Lord God, I pray that my child would be wise and quick to listen. Let him add to his learning, develop discernment, and gain guidance.*

### Pray that your child will develop a good work ethic.

In Ecclesiastes, Solomon repeatedly talked about the value of work and the importance of enjoying one's job (see Eccles. 2:24; 3:22; and 5:19). In the New Testament, the apostle Paul also taught the importance of our daily work. He told us that whatever we did, we should do it with all our hearts as a gift to the Lord (see Col. 3:23). He challenged the Thessalonian believers to live quiet lives and to work with their hands (see 1 Thess. 4:11). He also warned them against idleness, saying that if a man was unwilling to work, he shouldn't eat (see 2 Thess. 3:10).

Start praying early for your child's work ethic. Whether it's making his bed, feeding the dogs, mowing the yard, or doing homework, your child needs to learn that good, hard work is part of a God-honoring lifestyle. A kid who doesn't know the value and importance of work isn't set up to win when he becomes an adult. A lazy kid grows into a lazy adult. A kid with a sense of entitlement becomes an adult who feels that the world owes him a living.

Pray that your child will learn early how to work hard and to carry responsibility. Pray also that you will resist the temptation to coddle him or to look the other way when he isn't willing to fulfill his obligations or work where he's expected to. Model a good work ethic for him, and then teach him to have the same. Pray Colossians 3:23 for your child: *Father, I pray that my child will work willingly and joyfully, knowing that the fruit of his hard work honors you.*

### Pray that your child will have godly friends.

When my wife was growing up, she had a close friend who was very committed in her relationship with God. The two were inseparable in school. They played together, spent the night at each other's houses, studied together, went shopping together, and were cheerleaders together. They also kept each other out of trouble. Susie credits their friendship with helping her to make wise choices as she was growing up. Throughout elementary, middle, and high school, as the temptations increased and as more of her friends were making bad choices, Susie knew that she had a friend who was standing with her in her commitment to the high road. There is no doubt that Susie and her friend helped each other avoid the traps that many young girls fall into.

Sociologists tell us the influence of peers in children's lives is the number one influence of their behavior. In their early, formative years, the influence of friends has even more impact than the moral boundaries that accompany faith. A Canadian study of peer influence found that the behavior of friends was the biggest influence in twelve- to fifteen-year-olds' decisions to use drugs or alcohol. Only 8 percent chose to use drugs on their own, without the pressure from a friend. Four-fifths of kids who had tried marijuana said they had done so because most or all of their friends had.[1] A recent US study showed that kids who believed their friends had had sex were much more likely to experiment with sex themselves than those who believed their friends had never had sex.[2]

Statistics also show that peer relationships can be a powerful positive influence in the lives of children and teens.[3] That's why you want to pray for your child's friendships. That's why you want to know your child's friends, have them in your home, and get to know their families. It's scary to think about, but there will be times when your child's friends will actually have more influence on your child's decisions than you do, and a bad influence can easily lead an otherwise moral kid astray. The apostle Paul stated this truth in succinct biblical language: "Do not be misled: 'Bad company corrupts good character'" (1 Cor. 15:33).

W e pray for our boys to have good friends who point them to God, and we pray that they will be good friends to others. We pray that they will be leaders who point others to God. We pray that they will make friends easily and be welcoming to others.

A praying dad

Again, I turn to the example of Daniel. He stayed faithful to God while in the midst of severe temptation in Babylon. But remember, Daniel wasn't alone. In his wisdom God sent three other equally committed young men with Daniel to Babylon. When Daniel heard that they were all going to be executed along with the other wise men of Babylon, he went home to his friends, and they prayed to God for their deliverance (see

Dan. 2:13–18). Later, when the king ordered everyone in Babylon to worship a golden statue, Daniel's three friends stood together and refused to commit idolatry. Would any of these young men have had the same courage and tenacity if they had been standing alone? There's no doubt that they gained strength from their shared commitment to God.

Pray for your child's friends. Pray that your son or daughter will have a large group of peers who love God and are highly committed to living for him. Pray that your child's friends will encourage him or her to stay faithful to God. Pray Psalm 119:63 for your child: *Father, please help my child to befriend and be influenced by those who fear you and who seek to follow your Word.*

### Pray that your child will honor God in sports and other activities.

A few years ago, my daughter made it to the state finals in track. She attended a relatively small, private high school. The school competed against other smaller schools from all over the state. My daughter wasn't competing against the fastest girls in the state, but it was still an honor for her to be invited.

On the day of the meet, I was a nervous wreck. My daughter, on the other hand, was very calm. She couldn't have cared less how the race went. That, of course, drove her anxious and former track-running father crazy. The race was the 300-meter hurdles. It's a long, grueling sprint with hurdles thrown in just to make it even more torturous. It's also painful to watch.

As the race began, I found that my prayer life had a sudden boost of energy: *O God, please make Emily fast! God, help her to clear that hurdle! Oh, she's last! Why is she in last place? Please help her to run faster! God, why is that girl in front so fast? I bet she takes steroids. Please make her fall on the next hurdle. O God, Emily's gaining! Make her run faster! Go, God, go!* On and on it went. I just blabbered and blabbered all these goofy prayers.

I wonder what God thinks when we pray like that. Needless to say, while my prayers lacked eternal significance, they didn't lack passion. I think God understands (and, thankfully, puts up with) a parent's impassioned prayer for his or her child's sporting performance.

But there is more to competition than winning. If we all pray for our kids to win all the time, most of us are going to end up very disappointed. What does God want for our kids to experience through activities like Little League, drama club, a debate tournament, or a spelling bee?

Simply stated, God wants our kids to honor him. Sports and other activities give young men and women of God the chance to conduct themselves and perform in such a manner that lets Christ shine through them. How your son responds when he makes or misses a free throw, or how your daughter reacts when her soccer team loses—again—can go a long way toward bringing glory to Christ. How your child treats teammates and competitors will also give them a chance to point to what's eternal.

It's okay for your child to want to win. There's nothing wrong with that. But more importantly, you want your child to seize the platform that sports and competition offer him and to do all he can to glorify God. So pray for your child's competitions. Pray that he will always compete fairly and honorably. Pray that your child will play hard and always give his best effort. Pray that he will honor coaches, support teammates, and respect opponents. Pray 1 Corinthians 10:31 for your child: *Father, I pray that whatever my child does, including sports and competitions, he will do for your glory.*

60

### *Pray that your child will respect authority.*

The list of authority figures that your child meets on a daily basis is endless—counselors, teachers, principals, coaches, tutors, pastors, friends' parents, and even police officers and other civil servants. How your kid reacts to and treats authority figures is a vivid indicator of how she'll respond to the authority of God.

In Romans 13, we're instructed to honor and obey our leaders, including government leaders, because they have been placed in authority by God. Our submission to them is a reflection of our submission to and trust in God. In verse 7, Paul echoed the teachings of Jesus when he wrote, "Give everyone what you owe him: If you owe taxes, pay taxes; if revenue, then revenue; if respect, then respect; if honor, then honor."

In 1 Peter, Peter underscored the sentiments of Jesus and Paul. He wrote, "Submit yourselves for the Lord's sake to every authority instituted among men: whether to the king, as the supreme authority, or to governors, who are sent by him to punish those who do wrong and to commend those who do right" (1 Peter 2:13–14). And in his first letter to Timothy, Paul even called for the church to pray for government leaders: "I urge, then, first of all, that requests, prayers, intercession and thanksgiving be made for everyone—for kings and all those in authority, that we may live peaceful and quiet lives in all godliness and holiness" (1 Tim. 2:1–2).

Unfortunately, these inspired biblical commands seem to have been lost on this culture. How many headlines have you read recently that tell of kids disobeying, mocking, and even physically attacking the people in authority over them? And in our recent history, when we had presidents whom many Christians didn't like or support, instead of being prayed for, they were openly attacked and even hated by many churchgoing people. What kind of example does that set for our children?

In Matthew 8, Jesus's encounter with a Roman centurion offered a profound insight into the importance of submission to authority. Acknowledging Jesus's authority and his power over sickness, the centurion said, "For I myself am a man under authority, with soldiers under me. I tell this one, 'Go,' and he goes; and that one, 'Come,' and he comes. I say to my servant, 'Do this,' and he does it" (v. 9). Jesus affirmed the man's faith and humility. The leadership principle in this passage is clear: only those who are *under* authority are qualified to be *over* others. Only those who submit are qualified to be submitted to.

If we want our kids to grow into good and capable leaders—men and women of authority—then they have to learn early on how to submit to and respect those in authority over them. They have to learn that obedience to God and the leaders he's placed in authority over them isn't optional.

Pray that your child will learn to respect, honor, and submit to her leaders. Pray that she'll always be respectful of elected officials, even those she disagrees with. Pray Romans 13:7 for your child: *Holy God, please help my child to be obedient to those in authority over her and to always give them appropriate levels of respect and honor.*

### A Verse to Pray for Your Child

Matthew 7:24: *Lord Jesus, help my child to hear your words and put them into practice, much like the wise man who builds his house on a secure foundation.*

# 6

# ALL GROWN UP

## PRAYING FOR YOUR CHILD'S SPIRITUAL MATURITY

Good spiritual behaviors rarely begin in adult-hood. If we want our kids to practice spiritual disciplines and to be spiritually mature as adults, then they need to begin learning when they're young. If they don't learn how to sustain their souls early on, they may never grow up into spiritual maturity. Perhaps that is why 70 percent of Protestants who went to church regularly while in high school quit attending by age twenty-three.[1] They simply have no foundation upon which to stand.

This sad reality was made painfully clear during a recent visit I made to a local coffeehouse. I had a late meeting and had stopped in to get a fresh cup of hot decaf. I was served by a pleasant twenty-year-old who was eager to chat. I quickly learned that she had grown up in a very conservative family in an equally conservative town and had attended a well-known, traditional church all her life. In her own words, when she turned eighteen she "couldn't get to Austin fast enough."

Perhaps I should explain.

My hometown of Austin, although the capital of Texas, is not a part of the Bible Belt. Austin remains one of the most unchurched, spiritually uncommitted cities in North America. The politics, vibe, and attitude of Austin resemble other well-known party or New Age towns (our unofficial town motto is "Keep Austin Weird") and are not consistent with what you might expect from the capital of one of the most conservative and churched states in the union.

The young barista quickly confessed that she hadn't been to church since she moved to Austin. No sooner had the word "church" left her mouth than we were joined by three other young female employees who wanted to add to the conversation. All had similar stories: each had grown up attending a church—Catholic, charismatic, and Baptist—and each couldn't wait to break away from the repressive, backward, and uncool lifestyle that their respective parents had forced on them in their childhood. And they were more than willing to express their relative disdain for the spiritual system that they once called home. Only two of the four actually still claimed to hold to their Christian beliefs. The other two just didn't see the point.

These were not kids who had grown up in remote areas with no Christian presence. These were young ladies who had been raised in what sounded like relatively healthy, Bible-believing, Bible-preaching churches. They had been active in student ministries and church choirs. They had attended Vacation Bible School and church camps. These girls were not faith illiterates. They could recite the Apostle's Creed and sing the words to many Christian hymns.

What they could not do, however, was give me one compelling reason for them to continue to practice their faith openly.

## A Funny Thing Happened on the Way to Adulthood

The four coffeehouse workers represent a significant number of Christian youth in our nation. Since more and more young people choose to stop attending church when they leave home, we as Christian parents need to be asking some tough questions: Are we under-teaching, under-training, and under-equipping our Christian youth? What makes kids who have been raised in what is supposedly the body of Christ want so much to break out at their first opportunity? How do we raise our kids to be godly, spiritually mature adults?

A little later in the book, I'll show you how to pray for your own spiritual maturity since you are your child's primary spiritual mentor. But in the remainder of this chapter, I'd like us to learn how to pray for our kids' spiritual development. If we're going to be a nation of spiritually mature adults, then we've got to start producing spiritually mature kids. We certainly need to train and equip our kids to be godly, Christ-centered people. But most importantly, I believe, we need to pray for their spiritual development.

Following are six pinpoint prayers you can pray for your child's maturity. These aren't the only things that will help him or her grow up spiritually, but I believe they are foundational for equipping godly young kids to become even godlier adults.

### Pray that your child will see God as his heavenly Father.

"It looks as if the courts will have to decide who the real father of the baby is. With at least two men claiming paternal rights to the child, and with DNA testing still inconclusive, the matter may soon end up in the hands of a judge." As the reporter continued on with the story about the latest celebrity paternity suit, I couldn't help but think about the tragedy of that child's situation. Fatherhood isn't supposed to be a fuzzy area. Dads are meant to be known, not guessed at. God never intended that the question "Will my real dad please stand up?" be one that any child should have to ask, but each year more and more children are born into the world with the very strong possibility of never knowing their biological father. It's a cultural tragedy and a disgrace.

Believe it or not, there is a worse condition that affects even more kids each year. Millions and millions of kids grow up without ever knowing their *heavenly* Father. They may know about God, but they haven't made the connection that he is indeed their "Wonderful Counselor, Mighty God, Everlasting Father, Prince of Peace" (Isa. 9:6). Thus, we see generation after generation of spiritual orphans grow into confused and spiritually aimless adults, because they don't know the eternal God who is also their perfect Father.

Our inspiration for praying that our kids will know God as their Father comes from the Lord Jesus himself. The writer Luke tells us that when Jesus was only twelve, he stayed behind in Jerusalem after his parents had gone there for the annual Passover celebration. When the caravan of Jesus's family left for home, his parents assumed that he was somewhere in their group. It took them three days to find him still at the temple in Jerusalem, where he was discussing matters of faith and the law with the religious elders. When his parents asked him why he had stayed behind, he responded, "Why were you searching for me? . . . Didn't you know I had to be in my Father's house?" (Luke 2:49).

Jesus offered a very spiritually astute answer at what many of us would consider a young age. But a twelve-year-old child wasn't considered as young in first-century Hebrew culture. Jesus would have been thought of as a young adult. What he showed us in his comments was his undivided heart for God. Even though he was being raised by his earthly (but not biological) father, Joseph, Jesus had no doubts about where his loyalties ultimately lay. By his own confession, Jesus viewed his first priority as serving God. His reason: God was his Father; God's house was his Father's house; God's business was his Father's business.

Young Jesus's answer is a great pinpoint prayer you can offer for your own kid. Pray that, like Jesus, your child will know who his true Father is. Pray that he will be hungry and thirsty for his Father's presence. Pray that he will love God's house, work, Word, and mission.

A child who recognizes God as his heavenly Father will be well equipped to handle the times his earthly parents fail even when they have the best of intentions. Kids who sense that God has an unconditional, fatherly love for them typically feel secure enough to stand up under peer pressure and the relentless cultural pull toward compromise. Boys and girls who know God as their Father frequently grow into adults with passionate hearts for God. Let me give you an example.

I met Mallory on a recent flight to Denver. The twenty-one-year-old sat down next to me and within five minutes had identified herself as a believer. I tried to stay undercover and act like a nonbeliever (something I love to do to see how good Christians are at sharing their faith), but she quickly pegged me as a fellow Christ-follower. We had a delightful conversation for the remainder of the flight.

Mallory's faith and confidence in God inspired me. So did her passion to obey him. She was smart and articulate but had opted out of attending college. She simply didn't feel released by God to do what most of her friends were doing and what many adults expected her to do. She also didn't date—again, not because she didn't have any suitors, she just didn't feel God's permission. She was currently praying about where God might be directing her life. She was totally at peace with his will.

Mallory is a young woman who knows and loves her heavenly Father. Her parents have done a great job training and preparing her to function as an independent adult. They also have made sure she knows who her real Father is. The impact of their discipling and pinpoint praying for their daughter is obvious.

Start praying today that your child will understand that he has a Father in heaven who loves him and is always with him. Pray that he'll know that God is his best source of hope, strength, forgiveness, guidance, and courage and that he will be there for him even when you can't be. Pray that your child will feel secure enough in his relationship with God to humble himself before others. Pray also that he will have an unquenchable desire to be about his Father's business. Pray Psalm 2:7 for your child: *Father God, please call my child your child, and help him to call you his Father.*

### Pray that your child will love God's Word.

King David wrote, "Oh, how I love your law! I meditate on it all day long" (Ps. 119:97). Can you imagine your kid saying that to you? David also wrote, "How can a young man keep his way pure? By living according to your word" (Ps. 119:9). How would you feel if your nine-year-old son told you one night over dinner, "Hey, I'm praying that I will keep my way pure by always following God's Word." Would you pass out? Would you ask, "Who are you, and what have you done with my son?" Or what if your daughter asked you to help her memorize Bible verses so that she could hide God's Word in her heart and not sin against him (see Ps. 119:11)? Would you be willing to join her in her discipline?

Kids who love God's Word aren't fictional. They're not members of your fantasy family. They really do exist. And if you pray for your kids, they might just learn to love God's Word too.

David didn't fall in love with God's Word in his adulthood. We know from the account of his battle with Goliath that he had a profound faith and confidence in God even in his early years (see 1 Samuel 17). I'm sure David spent many long evenings alone out in a field, watching over his father's sheep, meditating on the law of Moses, and writing psalms and prayers to God. And in those moments with God, David fell in love with God's teachings.

In fact, nine times in Psalm 119, David talks about his outright love for God's Word (see vv. 47, 48, 97, 113, 119, 127, 159, 163, and 167). Wouldn't you be thrilled to know that your child loved the Scriptures? How would you feel if your kid viewed the Bible as God's liberating guide for living life well, not as just a restrictive set of rules? Pray that God will make your child hungry for his Word.

Children and young people who love the Scriptures will be well equipped to make good choices and live godly lives. They'll be more likely to have a servant's heart and an others-centered mind-set. They will learn to pursue wisdom and will frequently be wiser and more spiritually intuitive than their peers and even the adults who lead them (see Ps. 119:99–100; Prov. 1:1–6).

They will also learn to think biblically. They'll learn how to filter the information and opportunities culture throws at them through God's Word. They'll begin to look at the world from God's perspective. Such biblically thinking Christ-followers are exactly what our culture needs. Your child can be part of that next generation of leaders who helps turn our country back toward God. Pray that he will love God's Word. Pray that he will learn to think and process information from a biblical standpoint.

During my junior year in high school, I fell in love with the Bible. I was just ambushed by it. My suspicion is that my mother and several other godly adults were in cahoots together, praying for just such a spiritual ambush. I certainly needed one. Whatever it was, I quickly developed an insatiable hunger for God's Word. I couldn't get enough of it. I remember staying at home on Friday nights instead of going out with my friends so I could catch up on my Bible reading. I still have the old King James Bible that I read so diligently during my last two years of high school. Just about every page has verses underlined and notes written by a teenage boy whose heart had been totally apprehended by the Scriptures.

I'm not special, and I'm certainly not an isolated example. Pray that your child will love the Bible. Pray that he'll love to read it, meditate on it, memorize it, and study it. Pray Psalm 119:97 for your child: *Father, help my child to love your Word and to meditate on it day and night.*

> We love to pray, and it is the fiber that knits us together. We pray for the hurting, needy, elderly, or handicapped person in the grocery store. We pray at every automobile accident and for ambulances and fire trucks that pass us. We pray before tests and games. We pray for the hearts of bullies. We pray that God would build his kingdom in our hearts and make us mighty warriors for him. We pray for the hunger to serve and love God, to live lives worthy of Christ's place in our hearts, and to be servant leaders. We pray that we are extravagant lovers of Christ.
>
> A praying mom

### Pray that your child will love prayer.

Prayer is the currency of God's kingdom. Prayer is how we, as kingdom citizens, get things done. For your child to be a kingdom-minded person, for her to have authority and impact on a spiritual level, she has to be a person of prayer.

For many of us, good prayer skills don't come naturally. As important as prayer is in the life of Christ-followers, many still aren't really comfortable with it. Its quietness is intimidating, its intimacy frightening. But we don't have to settle for mediocre prayer lives for ourselves or for our children. The best way to add fuel to the fire of a struggling prayer discipline is to pray about it. Even if you can muster only a couple of minutes a day for prayer, make sure you spend part of that time asking God to help you, your spouse, and your child to become praying people. God will honor your request.

God gave Isaiah a beautiful promise that is also a great pinpoint prayer for your child. In Isaiah 56:7 God said, "These I will bring to my holy mountain and give them joy in my house of prayer. Their burnt offerings and sacrifices will be accepted on my altar; for my house will be called a house of prayer for all nations." In the context of that passage, God promised to extend his salvation well beyond the borders of Israel. He promised that foreigners who sought him would find him. You might recognize that Jesus quoted part of this verse when he rebuked the money changers in the temple (see Matt. 21:13).

I've always loved that God promised to bring us to his holy mountain, as the mountain symbolizes his presence. But my favorite line is the next one, where God promised to make us joyful in his house of prayer. I have prayed that verse for my family, my church, and myself for many years. I pray that we would love to pray and that it would be easy and natural for us. I pray that when our minds are at rest, or that when we have free time, our thoughts would drift toward prayer.

I've seen God answer these pinpoint prayers in beautiful ways. My kids are learning the value and importance of prayer. They're not afraid of it. My wife is a praying woman. The church I lead is filled with praying people, and prayer is a vital part of our decision-making process. Personally, I'm still not a good intercessor. I struggle with focusing and giving my best efforts to prayer. But prayer is never far from my mind. And

I can honestly say that I love praying, especially with others. God really has made me joyful in his house of prayer.

Pray the same for your child. Pray that she will be hungry for time with God. Pray that she will feel comfortable praying and won't feel intimidated in talking to God. Pray that intercession will be as natural for her as breathing. Ask God to help her develop a lifetime discipline of meeting with, talking to, and listening to him. Pray that as he answers her prayers, she will be motivated to pray for bigger things and her faith will grow.

Pray Isaiah 56:7 for your child: Father, I pray that you would bring my child to your holy mountain and that she would love being in your presence. I pray that she would feel great joy and satisfaction when she prays. Help her to see the impact she's having in your kingdom through her prayers. I pray that her sacrifices of praise and thanksgiving would always please you. Help her to always be part of a community of intercessors and to love your house of prayer.

### Pray that your child will hate sin.

The Bible tells us that every person has been wonderfully created in God's image. Being made in God's image means several things, not the least of which is the fact that we have a built-in capacity to know right from wrong. We have a natural moral compass. When a child is raised in a healthy spiritual environment, and when she is exposed to good teaching and modeling by her parents, her natural instinct is to begin to discern right from wrong.

Start praying while your child is young that she will have a clear sense of right and wrong. Pray that she will understand the concept of sin and that she'll have a healthy fear of it. Pray that your child will have the courage to recognize temptation when it comes calling and the courage to run from it.

Those prayers may not seem so relevant if your child is at a tender age, but be certain that temptation and sin are never far off, even for a young child. Satan is already making plans to try to steer her away from God. You need to counter those plans by praying for your child to learn to hate sin. Prayers for your child today will pay off later when she is confronted with temptation.

When I was in elementary school, I rode my bike to a nearby grocery store to look at the magazines and comics on display. While I was there, a man who seemed very friendly approached me. He told me that he had some really cool pictures back at his house that he wanted to show me. He then asked me if I wanted to go home with him. I remember an alarm going off inside of me right then. Something within me said, "Run away!" in a voice I could not miss. I turned away from the man, left the store, and rode home as fast as I could, scared but unscathed. I have no doubt that my mother's instructions and incessant prayers for me to recognize and run from temptation paid off for me that day.

Start today making prayer deposits in your child's spiritual bank account. They'll pay off someday. Pray that your child will know right from wrong and will see sin for what it really is. Pray Psalm 97:10 for your child: *Father, I pray that my child would love you and hate evil. Guard her life and deliver her from the hand of the wicked.*

### Pray that your child will know and use her spiritual gifts.

This is an embarrassing story for me to share, but it makes my point all too clearly. I was the pastor of a small church in a large denomination. I was working on a master's degree at a large seminary. I had been raised in a good church and had been very active in its student ministry my last two years of high school. But one day while leading a brief discussion with church leaders, I was asked what particular spiritual gifts I had that equipped me for ministry. I was absolutely stumped. I was a pastor, a seminarian, and a lifelong Christian, and not only did I not know my gifts, I had never even heard of the concept.

Every week I look at the new member cards for our church. I like to read about the journeys of faith that have brought so many new people to our fellowship. I am saddened to see, however, that many believers who come to us from other churches have no idea what their spiritual gifts are. How is it that so many churches have failed to embrace the importance of helping Christians identify and utilize their spiritual gifts? A Christian who doesn't know his gifts is the spiritual equivalent of a professional athlete who doesn't know his position or his sport.

As praying Christian parents, we need to pray that our kids will have opportunities to discover, develop, and utilize their spiritual gifts. If you don't know what your own gifts are, put this book down, go to your nearest Christian bookstore, and purchase one of the great resources available. Or just go online, google "spiritual gifts survey," and take a few of the online surveys you'll find. Start learning today about how God has specifically wired you for ministry in and to his body. Then start teaching your child. She needs to know that not only has God uniquely gifted her for service in his kingdom, but he will also hold her accountable for her stewardship of her gifts.

Recently I sat down with a group of high school students from our church who were preparing for a mission trip to a foreign country. Part of their training was to study the biblical passages that teach about gifts, complete two separate gift inventories, and then report back on what they believed their gifts to be. It was thrilling to hear these young believers talk about how excited they were that God had given them gifts such as teaching, leadership, mercy, discernment, service, hospitality, giving, prophecy, evangelism, and exhortation, and how they could see God using their various gifts in their lives for his kingdom causes. They even took assignments for the mission trip based on what gifts they had.

I was blown away. It's humbling to think what God will do with godly, sold-out young people who know that he has uniquely gifted them and wants to use them to bless and serve others. Pray that for your child. Pray that she'll start thinking at an early age about God's specific gifting and thumbprint on her life. Talk with your child about the gifts she may have and help her understand how she can use them for God's glory. Pray that she will take advantage of every opportunity to use, grow, and sharpen her spiritual gifts. Pray 1 Corinthians 12:1, 7 for your kid: *Father, I pray that my child will not be ignorant concerning spiritual gifts. Teach her to use her gifts as a manifestation of your Spirit for the common good of your church.*

### Pray that your child will love to worship God.

If prayer is the currency of God's kingdom, worship is the kingdom's love language. Where prayer moves God's Spirit, worship attracts God's presence. God is most at home in an atmosphere of praise.

Isaiah 6 and Revelation 4 and 5 show us what the interior of heaven looks like. Simply stated, it's filled with the praise and worship of God. Psalm 22:3 tells us that God is enthroned on the praises of his people. When Paul and Silas added worship to their prayers in a Philippian jail cell, God's Spirit landed in the midst of their praise, the walls of the prison were shaken, and everyone's chains fell off (see Acts 16:25–26). That's what happens when we develop a life of worship—people's chains fall off.

Too many Christians are uninformed or immature when it comes to worship. We don't know its potential, and we don't understand how it transforms lives. We get more exuberant and expressive at a high school football game than we do in a church service. We're more passionate about checking the winning lotto numbers each week than we are about proclaiming the riches and majesty of God. For many of us, worship is "the stuff that happens before preachin.'"

If you want to raise a true kingdom-building kid, then pray that she would fall in love with worshiping Jesus. Few things can teach a young Christ-follower the reality and power of God more than worship. Psalm 33:1 declares that it is fitting for the upright to praise God. Psalm 84:10 teaches that it would be better to spend one day in the courts of the Lord in worship than a thousand days anywhere else. And in John 4:23–24, Jesus taught that God actually seeks men and women who will worship him in spirit and in truth. God wants worshipers. Pray that your child will be one.

Recently, at one of our church's worship nights, I had a ringside seat to a great parenting moment between a mom and her son. Our worship team was onstage, leading us in a season of extended time of praise through song. One of our vocalists was quietly and reverently lifting one of her hands to God in a gesture of praise. I noticed that a young boy of about nine, who was standing between his parents, raised one of his hands. It was a little humorous because he raised his hand straight up, like he wanted to ask a question. But it was clear that the young man was imitating what he saw the vocalist doing.

After a minute or so, his mom noticed that he had his hand in the air. I watched as she bent down and began to whisper in his ear. She talked to him for a long time, maybe even for a full minute. When she started talking, the boy lowered his hand and began listening intently. Occasionally he would nod his head, as if he understood what his mother was saying.

Finally, the mom pulled away and began singing again. Her son stood for a long time with his hands resting on the seat in front of him. But a few minutes later, without being prompted by anyone, that young worshiper raised his hand back into the air.

That was one of the coolest, sweetest, most unforgettable parenting moments that I'd seen in a long time. I don't know what the young boy was thinking or feeling, but I pray that he was getting a taste of what it means to rush headlong into loving Jesus.

Pray that your child will love to worship. Ask God to make her comfortable in worship and praise. Pray that she would rather spend an hour worshiping Christ than doing anything else. Pray that she will see the power and blessing of corporate worship. Pray Psalm 122:1 for your child: *Lord, I pray that my child will rejoice and be glad when she has the opportunity to worship in your house.*

Finally, pray for the next generation. Pray that God will raise up a holy generation of fearless young worshipers. Pray that we who are now adult believers will seize the moments God gives us to teach our kids about the power of blessing God. Pray that we will be mature and comfortable in praise so that we can teach and train our kids how to worship the Lord. Pray Isaiah 43:21 for us as adults and for the next generation: *Father, make us a people that show forth your praise!*

## A Verse to Pray for Your Child

Ephesians 1:17: *Lord Jesus, I pray that you will give my child a spirit of wisdom and revelation, so that she might know you better.*

# 7

## Pinpoint Prayers for the Man Your Son Will Become

I couldn't believe this was actually happening. Even as I spoke the words, they didn't seem real, couldn't be real: "My son is lost in the mountains!" The young park ranger knew immediately that I was serious. She quickly ushered me to a back room where she gave me some water, took down the necessary information, and then radioed for an all-out search for my son. I've never in my life felt so helpless or afraid. *Dear God, you can see my son right now. You know where he is. Please guide him to safety. Please protect him.*

The day had started innocently enough. My son, Will III, and I were hiking with a few other people in the Mummy Range just northwest of Estes Park, Colorado. If the weather behaves, ambitious hikers can actually summit anywhere from three to six peaks in one day in the Mummies. Our party was aiming for three summits. We had successfully climbed two thirteen-thousand-foot peaks, and we were on our way to the third and easiest of the three when the trouble began.

Will was having the best climb of his young life. My then thirteen-year-old son had figured out that he loved hiking. He was in great shape and had just about sprinted up the first two mountains, leaving me far behind. I'd kept my eye on Will, but I had also given him a long leash. I wanted him to enjoy the day and forever be hooked on climbing.

We took a short break on the summit of the second mountain, a sloping beauty known as Chiquita. While I was making small talk with a couple we'd met on the summit, Will asked me if he could start hiking toward our third and final peak of the day, Mount Chapin. I had hiked from Chapin to Chiquita and back on several occasions, though never alone as a thirteen-year-old. But I remembered it being easy and safe. I told Will to go ahead (we could see Chapin's summit where we were standing) and that I would catch up to him shortly. I left the summit in pursuit of my son no more than two minutes later. I never found him.

At thirteen thousand feet, there are no trees to block the line of sight. I should have been able to spot Will immediately, even if he was several hundred yards ahead of me. But I couldn't. He was nowhere to be seen. We were carrying walkie-talkies, so I quickly tried to reach Will on his. We spoke for only a few seconds because something was blocking our signals. I could tell that he was okay physically, but I couldn't discern where he was.

I retraced my steps back up to the summit of Chiquita. I wanted to determine if there was any way I could have missed seeing Will or if he could have somehow taken a wrong turn. Bear in mind that I had already climbed two thirteen-thousand-foot peaks that day. Retracing my steps was no easy effort, and it took me nearly twenty minutes to regain the summit I had left only a few minutes before. There was no sign of Will. It was like he had vanished into the thin mountain air.

Suddenly I was very afraid. My thirteen-year-old son was somewhere out there in the mountain wilderness, alone. He had only enough food and water for a one-day hike. It was afternoon, the time of day when thunderstorms bring lightning and hard rains to the high altitudes. We were also high enough for the temperatures to dip well below freezing at night. Added to that were the ever-present threats of the mountain lions and bears that roam the area. My son was in trouble, and I knew it.

I had one final hope. I thought that maybe Will had given up on his effort to climb Chapin, found the trail, and headed back to the parking lot, knowing that he would eventually meet us there. Realizing that was my last real shot at finding him, I left our hiking party and ran the three miles from Chiquita's summit to the trailhead and parking area down below. As I rounded the final turn that would take me to the paved parking area, I silently prayed that my son would be there. I can't describe the pain that I felt in my gut when I found the parking lot empty. Will wasn't there. He hadn't yet come down the mountain.

I then made one of the most difficult decisions I've ever made in my life. I got in my car and drove away from the mountain. It took me nearly an hour to drive to the nearest ranger station. I was miles away from my son. I couldn't reach him or help him. I wasn't even sure where he was. My son was lost.


**Lord, Save My Son!**

During the long minutes of the gut-wrenching drive to the ranger station, I had a lot of time to pray and think. The script in my mind read something like this:

>**Prayer:** *O God, you can see my son right now. Please lead him to safety.*

81

**Thought:** *How could I be so stupid? I can't believe I let him wander off alone.*

**Prayer:** *Dear Jesus, please keep the bears and mountain lions away from him.*

**Thought:** *I wonder how his food is holding up. I wonder if he has enough water.*

**Prayer:** *O God, I'm so sorry. Please forgive me for losing my son, your son.*

**Prayer:** *God, please protect my son. Meet him right there on that mountain and keep him safe!*

**Prayer:** *Father, if you'll save my son, I'll never leave him alone again.*

**Thought:** *When do I tell his mother? What do I tell his mother? "Sorry, honey, but I lost our son in a wild and vast forest. Don't worry; I'm sure he'll be fine!"*

**Thought:** *I won't tell her. I'll move to Sri Lanka.*

**Prayer:** *O God, please give Will the sense to find his way to safety.*

On and on it went—prayers, pleadings, thoughts, confessions, and fears. My mind was one big jumbled mess. It was all I could do to pray. It required all my energy and focus. And yet I never stopped praying. I knew that God could see my son right then and there on that mountain, in that wilderness. While I may have been powerless to help my son, God wasn't. Prayer wasn't just the best option I had, it was the only option.

### It's a Jungle Out There

There's no doubt that our sons face a plethora of temptations and obstacles to godliness. The wildernesses they travel in are vast, deep, and filled with danger. The threats my son encountered on the mountain are mild compared to the spiritual land mines that are buried all around our sons. In today's day and age, it really takes only one misstep to devastate a life.

In this chapter, I want to help you learn how to pray for your son. I want you to start praying today that he'll successfully find his way through the wildernesses that lie before him. The topics that I have chosen to address may surprise you. But as a man who has ministered to men for over twenty years, I can assure you that these are relevant pinpoint prayers that you can pray for your son for years to come.

### Pray that your son will crave Christian community.

Men need community. They need the fellowship of other strong, believing men to keep them on the high road. We've all heard the devastating true stories of men who chose to do life alone and then crashed and burned.

Aron Ralston knows all about the dangers of going solo. In April of 2003, the young mountain climber chose to go climbing alone in Utah's Blue John Canyon. He didn't tell anyone where he was going. After an eight-hundred-pound boulder fell on his arm, crushed his hand, and pinned him to the mountain wall, Ralston spent six days trying to survive and hoping for rescue. It never came. Finally, battling hyperthermia and dehydration, Ralston took out a small knife, cut off his right hand, somehow managed to rappel eighty feet to the canyon floor below, and then hiked out to freedom.

Ralston knows that his isolationist mind-set almost cost him his life. He wrote, "I realized that my situation was the result of decisions that I had made. I chose to go out there by myself. I chose to not tell anybody where I was going."[1] Ralston's near miss is a graphic example of what can happen when a person chooses to hike alone.

Doing life alone is even more dangerous. Let me be clear: a man can be surrounded by people—friends, family, co-workers—and still be alone. Aron Ralston was physically alone. Many other men choose to be relationally alone. They never learn to let anybody in.

The trend toward isolation starts when we're young. Our culture doesn't encourage boys and young men to pursue authenticity, intimacy, and relational connection. Our heroes are celebrated for their athletic skills or for millions earned, battles won, or women had. Few men ever make headlines for having meaningful conversations with a friend or confessing a struggle to an accountability partner. And yet those are precisely the types of behaviors honored in Scripture and required for boys to become healthy, emotionally stable adults. Isolation breeds sin, shame, and eventually death. Community—relational authenticity and commitment—breeds spiritual and emotional maturity. Start praying today for your son to know the joys of living in Christian community. Pray that he'll choose to have open, accountable friendships with other godly men.

The Bible is loaded with examples of men who were committed to living life against the backdrop of authentic community. To some degree, the men who lived in the centuries preceding Christ and even Christ's contemporaries were better set up to win than most men today. Our pacing and cultural norms work against us developing real friendships. But the examples are there in the Scriptures, and they make good fodder for pinpoint prayers for your son's relational community.

Consider Jonathan and David. Their friendship is a strong example of two healthy males who knew how to really go deep with each other. In today's dysfunctional culture, their relationship would be greeted with cynicism and sarcasm, to say the least. Men today just don't have friendships in which they cry together, defend each other, hunt and fish together, fight together, and openly embrace, without somebody getting suspicious. But there was nothing odd about how David and Jonathan lived.

Jesus modeled a similar level of intimacy with his disciples, specifically Peter, James, and John. Paul's letters are filled with the names of people whom he loved dearly and prayed for regularly. He openly prayed to God for the chance to travel and visit his friends.

You want your son to learn early in life the value of Christian community. Here's why:

- *Community increases accountability.* It's hard to wander too far off course when you're walking through life with a pack of godly men. Community will help keep your son on the high road.
- *Community encourages confession and forgiveness.* When your son stumbles in sin, he's going to need a safe place to openly talk about his failure and find the healing and forgiveness he'll desperately need. Lack of confession breeds secrecy and shame, and when those two are combined, they always lead to a duplicitous life. A healthy Christian community will give your son a place to be honest about his struggles.
- *Community enhances spiritual growth.* Cyclists ride together and marathoners train together because they typically ride and run harder in a group than alone. Having a group of hot-hearted Christians around your son will push him in his Christian walk. He's more likely to pray, fast, serve, give, worship, and remain pure when he's surrounded by a group of guys who are seeking to do the same.

King David talked in the Psalms about the power of community and accountability. In Psalm 141:5 he wrote, "Let a righteous man strike me—it is a kindness; let him rebuke me—it is oil on my head. My head will not refuse it." David openly invited the admonishment and teaching of righteous men. He knew firsthand the power of a godly rebuke delivered in love (see 2 Sam. 12:1–10). In Psalm 101, David talked about the kind of men he wanted to spend time with: "Men of perverse heart shall be far from me; I will have nothing to do with evil. Whoever slanders his neighbor in secret, him will I put to silence; whoever has haughty eyes and a proud heart, him will I not endure. My eyes will be on the faithful in the land, that they may dwell with me; he whose walk is blameless will minister to me. No one who practices deceit will dwell in my house; no one who speaks falsely will stand in my presence" (vv. 4–7).

There's one more thing to remember when praying for your son to value community. The type of authentic relationships that David, Jonathan, Paul, and Jesus modeled rarely happens by accident. If your son is going to know how to be relationally real, then he needs to learn it from you. Don't expect your son to make community a priority if you don't. Don't expect him to have good relational skills and deep friendships if you don't. And don't expect him to be willing to submit to the accountability of another Christian if you're not. In other words, if you want your son to be equipped to do relationships well, then you've got to show him how.

Pray that your boy will be open to intimate and authentic friendships. Pray that he'll give godly friends, mentors, a godly spouse, and, most of all, Jesus access to his heart. Pray Matthew 26:36–38 for your child: *Father, I pray that my son will be like Jesus. I pray that he will surround himself with godly men. I pray also that even in his deepest times of pain, he will seek the company and prayers of godly men.*

### *Pray that your son will pursue sexual purity.*

The man who sat before me was a broken shell of the man I once knew. I was teaching at a Christian retreat for some high school kids. During one of the breaks, a man whom I had known for years approached me and asked if we could talk. It didn't take long for his pain, grief, and shame to come spilling out. He confessed that he was addicted to pornography.

His habit had started in the usual way. When he was a kid he used to sneak peeks at his dad's "hidden" copies of *Playboy*. He continued his habit through his adolescent and college years but never really thought much about it. He certainly didn't think it was sin. As he became an adult and a well-known business leader, his addiction increased. Porn became the drug he'd use to escape the realities of business stress and a struggling marriage. But soon his *Playboy* habit became a playboy lifestyle. No longer content to look, the man began to act on his impulses. Monthly trips to "gentlemen's clubs" became weekly. Flirtation became encroachment. Late-night business meetings grew into one-night stands. And a formerly faithful marriage became riddled with infidelity.

As the man shared his story with me, he made a comment that shook me. After confessing all his junk and sin, he said quietly, "I think my addiction has found its way to my son." You know the scariest part of this story? That was in the mid-1980s—*before* the Internet, before any boy or man could access porn on his personal computer.

### A Call to Arms

We live in a day where the opportunities for sexual exploration, sexual confusion, sexual abuse, and sexual addiction exist at levels unmatched in human history. The advent of the Internet, with all the potential for good that it brings, has also produced new and tremendously easy opportunities for sin. Today, any young man with a computer can search for, read about, view pictures and videos of, and talk with proponents for and participants in just about every form of sexual expression and deviation you can think of—and many more you don't want to. We have yet to see the true impact on a society filled with hormonally rich young men who have been raised on a diet of on-demand sexual fantasy and stimulation. But we're about to, and we can be sure of this—it's not going to be pretty.

I believe that the redefining of sexual standards and norms may be the single greatest threat to our culture today. It has a frighteningly familiar feel of the descent into depravity described so vividly by Paul in Romans 1:18–32. And in the bull's-eye of this threat are boys and young men.

Christian parents, don't be naive. Your son will have countless opportunities to succumb to sexual temptation in its various forms throughout his life—more temptations, quite frankly, than any generation of men before him. And since you can't put a leash around his neck or keep him in a sterile bubble the rest of his life, you'd better get busy praying for him. The best weapon you have in the battle for your son's sexual purity is pinpoint prayer.

### Run Away

The book of the Bible most dedicated to the teaching of wisdom is Proverbs. The thoughts, collections, and sayings of Solomon, arguably the wisest man in history, are offered in Proverbs for all who would seek to live wisely. I find it very interesting, almost ironic, that the book of the Bible most dedicated to the propagation of wisdom begins with several chapters warning of the folly of sexual sin. I find it even more intriguing that these warnings are offered by the son of a known adulterer.

Solomon grew up in a household that formed as the result of sexual sin. Murder, conspiracy, lies, the death of an innocent child, and decades of war and extreme family conflict became brutal realities in David's life as a result of his adulterous actions. Solomon, having witnessed firsthand the devastation that such behavior brings, committed the first portion of his wisdom collection to teaching young men about the need for sexual purity. Listen to his words:

It [wisdom] will save you also from the adulteress, from the wayward wife with her seductive words, who has left the partner of her youth and ignored the covenant she made before God. For her house leads down to death and her paths to the spirits of the dead. None who go to her return or attain the paths of life.

Proverbs 2:16–19

For the lips of an adulteress drip honey, and her speech is smoother than oil; but in the end she is bitter as gall, sharp as a double-edged sword. Her feet go down to death; her steps lead straight to the grave.

Proverbs 5:3–5

Drink water from your own cistern, running water from your own well.

Proverbs 5:15

May your fountain be blessed, and may you rejoice in the wife of your youth. A loving doe, a graceful deer—may her breasts satisfy you always, may you ever be captivated by her love.

Proverbs 5:18–19

Why be captivated, my son, by an adulteress? Why embrace the bosom of another man's wife?

Proverbs 5:20

89

So is he who sleeps with another man's wife; no one who touches her will go unpunished.

Proverbs 6:29

But a man who commits adultery lacks judgment; whoever does so destroys himself.

Proverbs 6:32

I could list several others.

Do you hear the passion in Solomon's pleas? Can you feel the pain of hard-learned lessons in his instructions? Aren't you glad the Holy Spirit led Solomon to include those teachings in Proverbs? Solomon has set a great example for us, and we would do well to be equally diligent in teaching our own sons about the sexual high road. Your diligence in teaching and praying for your son can be fueled by the knowledge that even though Solomon knew these lessons and taught them, he ultimately didn't listen to them. Solomon ended up losing his kingdom because he rejected his own counsel.

Don't hide these verses in Proverbs from your son. Read them to him, talk to him about them, and pray them over him.

> We pray every night that our kids are protected from evil at school, that they would be able to discern right from wrong and good from evil, and that they would be repulsed by things that are not of God.
>
> A praying mom

Also, pray that your son will be sexually pure until he's married. Pray that he will be afraid of sexual sin and that he will quickly run from it. Pray that he will respect women and always treat them with the same love and dignity that Jesus did. Pray that he will have friends and date girls who are equally committed to their own sexual purity. Pray that he will be repulsed when exposed to pornographic images. Pray that he will be immediately caught if he ever begins to practice any form of sexual sin. Pray Psalm 101:3 for your son: *Father, I pray that my son will never look upon a vile or profane image and that he will hate the deeds of faithless men.*

### Pray that your son will be willing to lead.

Bill is a great example of what I don't want my son to be like. Bill is married with three kids. He doesn't work. His wife makes a good living at her job, so he doesn't have to work. But I wouldn't really describe Bill as a stay-at-home dad. His kids are all in school, so he doesn't need to stay home all day. Beyond that, Bill's not particularly spiritual. The spiritual temperature of the family is clearly set by his wife.

In short, I'm not really sure what role Bill plays in his family. But one thing is obvious: he doesn't lead it.

Bill is a fictional example of a very real trend in our culture today. Men have totally surrendered their leadership role. I'm not saying that women can't and shouldn't lead; far from it. I am saying that men have a distinct and God-given assignment of leadership in culture and in their homes, but many have forfeited that assignment. They have surrendered their leadership, in some cases placing women in dual leadership roles they were not designed to fill.

Leadership, when most broadly defined, is simply influence. While all men aren't going to be presidents, elected officials, CEOs, or leaders of a nonprofit organization, they are supposed to lead their families and be people of impact in society. But many have dropped the ball, and as a result, our Western culture is facing a shortage of male leadership. Not a shortage of men—just male leaders.

I've seen it far too many times: The husband who is away on business more nights a year than he is home. The father who thinks his kids need church but he doesn't. The man who is intimidated by spiritual things and can't carry on a

91

meaningful conversation about God. The husband who can't hold a steady job and leans heavily on his wife for his own livelihood. The dad who spends more time over a beer than a Bible.

Young men and boys in our culture are growing up with many poor role models when it comes to true male leadership. From philandering politicians to steroid-taking sports heroes to absentee dads, our next generation of men is in desperate need of a God-given calling to be leaders. And as parents of that next generation of potential leaders, it's our job to pray that they get that calling.

Pray that your son will discover and embrace his God-given role to lead. It might be large or small, broad or narrow, but it is significant nonetheless. Here are three specific things to pray for your son's budding leadership role:

- *His vision.* Leadership comes out of vision, and every great leader has a sense of calling and vision. Pray that your son will have a clear awareness of where he is going and what God is doing with him. (We'll discuss this further in chapter 9.) Pray Jeremiah 1:5 for your son. Pray that he will know God created him for a special purpose and that he has been consecrated and set apart for God's mission.

- *His courage.* Leaders need courage. They need the emotional and spiritual gusto to stand firm in the face of personal and cultural opposition to doing what's right. As your son seeks to be a leader and set a good example, he will no doubt be told by well-meaning friends and even family, "Don't be so serious," "Have a little fun," "Take a chill pill," or "Don't take your faith so seriously." Men who lead can expect culture to push back, and the more they lead, the more intense the opposition will become. Pray that your son will always have the courage to do what's right. Pray Joshua 1:9 for him. Pray that he will be strong and courageous. Pray that he will never grow weary or become discouraged. Pray that he will know that God is with him wherever he goes.

- *His wisdom.* Leaders need wisdom. As your son grows, he will be faced with countless opportunities to make choices that will impact not only his life but the lives of others around him. As the leader of his family or business, or as a leader in his church or community, he will need wisdom to lead well. Pray that he will always seek and heed God's wisdom. Let the first three chapters of Proverbs guide you as you pray for your son's wisdom. Then pray James 1:5 for your son. Pray that God will freely and generously grant his wisdom to your son.

## Home

An hour after I reached the ranger station and reported Will missing, he made his way back to the main trail and found the others in our hiking party. When he had left the summit of Chiquita, he'd actually walked straight down a steep and dangerous face of the mountain, losing the trail in the process. There was a huge ridge between where Will went and where I was. Even though we were only a few hundred yards apart, there was no way I could have seen him.

My son had kept his wits about him. He'd used the sun to determine his bearings and then simply reversed his steps and hiked back up to where he started. Not a bad reaction for a thirteen-year-old. It took the party about two hours to hike down to the trailhead, where they could use a phone to call me. I've never been more thrilled, relieved, or grateful to God than I was when I heard Will's voice. My prayers had been answered. My son was okay. I was not going to have to move to Sri Lanka.

Will has spent the last two summers working for a Christian camp in Colorado, leading teenagers on hikes in the mountains, including the very same mountains he got lost in. God used his "lost" experience to refine and grow his character. And he used it to remind me of the importance of teaching, training, and praying for my children.

Start praying for your son right now. It's never too late for him to find his way home.

### A Verse to Pray for Your Son

1 Chronicles 12:8: *Lord, make my son a mighty man of valor. Train his heart and hands for spiritual battle. Give him a face like a lion and make him as swift and surefooted as a gazelle in the mountains.*

# 8

# PINPOINT PRAYERS FOR THE WOMAN YOUR DAUGHTER WILL BECOME

THERE'S NOTHING MORE beautiful than a young woman who walks with Christ. There is a quiet peace, confidence, and joy that radiate through the life of a girl whose first love is Jesus. Headlines and entertainment networks are filled with stories of wild women who think they somehow become more attractive and popular by living out-of-control, reckless lives. But actually, the opposite is true. Let me show you what I mean.

## A Three-Ring Ceremony

It was no doubt one of the coolest, most memorable wedding moments I've ever experienced. I was leading the wedding for a friend's daughter and her fiancé. I had enjoyed every minute of the months of preparation we'd done. I hate to admit this, but I've come to dread meeting with couples—even Christian couples—who want to get married. Typically they're not taking the high road: they're living and sleeping together and don't really think it's wrong. And since I won't marry a Christian couple who is doing either, I have to ask if they are, and that typically leads to a pretty bumpy meeting.

My friend's daughter, Sara, and her fiancé, Chris, were just the opposite. They were doing everything right. They had never slept together and had no intention of doing so until their wedding night. They were both very godly young people who seemed to genuinely love Jesus more than they loved each other. They prayed together, worshiped together, and served together. I didn't see how this couple could get any cooler. I was wrong. They totally blew me away at their wedding—actually, Sara did.

They had a three-ring ceremony. Sara had taken a pledge in her early teenage years to remain sexually pure until she was married. The pledge was part of a program on sexuality and holiness that her church had sponsored. As a symbol of her commitment to stay pure, Sara wore a ring on the ring finger of her left hand. It basically said to the world, "Hey, you see this ring? It means I'm married to Jesus. My heart, soul, and body belong to him. No one is going to have access to any of them until Jesus says it's okay."

During the ceremony, Sara took off that ring. She looked her man in the eyes, removed the ring, and handed it to him. She told him that she had kept herself pure for him. She told him that she had her fathers' (her dad's and Jesus's) permission to marry him. She told him that her pure and unadulterated body was his.

I'd never seen anything like it at a wedding. I'm sure I heard a collective *thump*—the sound of chins hitting the floor as the jaws of young men all over the room fell open. It was one of the most profound, most powerful, purest, and most tender wedding moments I'd ever seen. Sara is one of the most beautiful Christian young women I've ever met, and it has nothing to do with how she looks.

In this chapter, I want us to learn how to pray for our daughters to be beautiful Christian women. Let's learn how to seek God's favor on and protection for their lives. Let's learn to pray against the terrible pull of culture that says they have to look, act, and live a certain way to be accepted.

> Praying for my girls is a full-time job. I keep reminders around me so I'll constantly remember to say quick prayers for them. I keep pictures of them in my office, in my briefcase, and on the sun visor in my car. I carry a small angel in my pocket to remind me to pray for my girls.
>
> A praying dad

There are countless verses in the Bible that can become powerful pinpoint prayers for your daughter. I encourage you to always read your Bible with a pen in hand so that when you see a verse you want to start praying for your girl, you'll be ready to write her initials right next to it in the margin and begin to pray that verse. But here, let's zero in on some prayers that will be foundational as we pray for our girls.

### Pray that your daughter will love herself.

My wife, Susie, is one of the godliest, most secure women I've ever known. She grew up in a home with two parents who loved her and praised her often. More importantly, she was raised knowing that God loves her unconditionally. Whether she felt pretty or not, made good grades or not, or was popular or not, Susie always knew that God loved her. As a result, she has a healthy self-esteem.

Susie has been great for our daughters. She's been able to teach them from her own experience where their real value lies. She's also been able to teach them to love themselves.

Susie loves to sing. She often walks around the house singing little songs to herself. Lately she's been singing one to the tune of the old Beatles' song "She Loves You." You know the one. But Susie's version is a little different. It goes, "I love me, yeah, yeah, yeah." Like I said, my wife has a healthy self-image.

One of the oldest, most frequently taught commands in the Bible is for us to love our neighbor as we love ourselves (see Lev. 19:18). Jesus named this command as one of the two that best summed up the teachings of the law. We are the most godly, he taught, when we love others as we love ourselves (see Matt. 22:36–40).

The part of those verses that gets the most airtime by preachers and teachers is the "love your neighbor" part, for good reason. Jesus emphasized that kingdom citizens need to live with a strong, others-centered orientation. But the standard he gave for determining how we love others is often overlooked. Jesus taught that our love for others should mirror our love for ourselves. In other words, we should treat, care for, provide for, respect, and meet the needs of others exactly as we do ourselves.

Here's the problem: in today's world, few of us know what it means to love ourselves. It's a concept that seems almost vain or conceited. And when you mix in the cultural mandates that we have to look, act, dress, and live a certain way in order to really be hip, the potential for personal discontentedness only increases. In other words, it's typically not easy for people to really love themselves in today's world.

Do you know what segment of the population may have the most difficult time loving themselves? Young women. Today's girls and young women are bombarded with daily messages that inevitably make them feel that they don't measure up in some way. Godly parents will be savvy enough to pick up on these not-so-subtle messages, teach their girls otherwise, and pray for them to have a healthy self-love.

So here's the $64,000 question: what does it mean to love yourself? Specifically, what does it mean for a preadolescent or teenage girl to love herself? When you pray for your daughter to love herself, what are you really asking? Let's find out.

*When your daughter loves herself, she will know that she is fearfully and wonderfully made.* There's a well-known plastic surgeon in my hometown whose advertisements have been known to target teen girls. With comments such as, "We can get rid of those extra pounds," "You can have bigger breasts just in time for the homecoming dance (or prom)," and "Let us fix your figure flaws," he's clearly communicating to girls that their self-worth is very much wrapped up in how they look. Sadly, his message is getting through: business is booming.

The onslaught starts when they're young. Whether it's the Playboy-model shape of Barbie; the cartoon heroines complete with small waists, big breasts, and exposed midsections; the *Seventeen* magazine mind-set that blasts them with images and headlines of "Sex Tricks Your Guy Will Love" or "How to Have the Body You've Always Wanted"; or photos of celebrities who are thought to be overweight and are being ridiculed for it, our girls are bombarded with the message that if they're not sexy, well built, and using their body to get what they want, then they're not socially acceptable.

Too many Christian parents are discovering that their late elementary-age girls and, of course, their middle and high school girls struggle with purging, bulimia, and anorexia because they're afraid they're getting too big. As praying parents, we need to start combating these dangerous cultural messages when our girls are young. We need to teach them the truth about their true value and pray that they will believe God's truth, not culture's, about their worth.

The powerful words of Psalm 139 need to be etched into the heart of every young girl. Listen to them: "For you created my inmost being; you knit me together in my mother's womb. I praise you because I am fearfully and wonderfully made; your works are wonderful, I know that full well. My frame was not hidden from you when I was made in the secret place. When I was woven together in the depths of the earth, your eyes saw my unformed body. All the days ordained for me were written in your book before one of them came to be" (vv. 13–16).

Those verses teach that the way we were created should produce a sense of awe in us. We should look at ourselves and marvel at the skill and artistry that God demonstrated when he made each of us. They tell us that the Holy Spirit was busy long before we were born, working in us and on us. He formed not just our physical bodies but our personalities, our gift and skill sets, our mental abilities, and our emotional capacities.

Those words are true for every human being—regardless of gender, skin color, education, income, or morality (or lack thereof). Every soul is uniquely and beautifully crafted by God. To love yourself is to know that God did a wonderful thing when he made you.

For your daughter to love herself means that she knows her value and worth aren't based on how she looks or who her friends are. It means that she doesn't need a boyfriend or have to be homecoming queen to feel good about herself. A girl who believes she is fearfully and wonderfully made will be able to love herself more readily than one who looks in the mirror and doesn't like what she sees. Pray that your daughter will be in awe of what God did when he made her. Pray that she will know she is fearfully and wonderfully made.

*When your daughter loves herself, she will know that she is worth dying for.* In Romans 5:8 Paul tells us that Jesus was willing to die for us, even while we were sinners. God loved us enough, even in our sin and rebellion, to send his holy Son to die. People who know that will have a different understanding of what makes a person valuable.

That simple message of God's redemption and forgiveness in Jesus is the most life-giving and hope-producing message in the world. That message can give a girl who feels the need to conform to the cultural norms around her the courage to stand up and live a life of holiness for God. When she begins to see her true worth, when she realizes that she is valuable enough for the Son of God to die for—with or without makeup, a great figure, perfect nails, a cool boyfriend, the coolest clothes, and the hippest hair—then she will begin to feel confident enough in who she is in Christ to live for him, not what everyone around her says she should live for. Let me offer a real-life example.

Nicole, dressed head to toe in black, wanted to talk. That by itself could have been counted as a miracle. The counselors and staff of the youth camp where I was the guest pastor had noticed Nicole on the first day. Even among the five hundred high schoolers who were there, she was hard to miss. She wore the same thing every day to every event—black. Black shirt, black shoes, black pants, black fingernail paint, black overcoat. Her lovely face was pierced from side to side and top to bottom.

Nicole's attitude was as dark as her wardrobe. She claimed to be a witch, or an agnostic, or an atheist, or something else, depending on the day and her mood. Whatever she was, or thought she was, we knew better. Nicole was hurting. She was a sixteen-year-old carrying the hurt and pain of someone well beyond her years. She was also a perfect candidate for a Jesus ambush.

We started praying for Nicole early in the week. No one actually knew how she had ended up at a Christian camp, but we knew she was there for a reason. So we asked God to introduce her to his Son. And when she asked if she could stay after a service and talk, I wasn't totally surprised. Thrilled, but not surprised.

Nicole's story wasn't all that unusual—a broken home, a disappearing dad, a lost and hurting mom, and lots of sex, drugs, and rock and roll as pain killers. They hadn't worked. Nicole listened intently as I told her about Jesus's love. She'd heard it before. But this time something was different. Nicole seemed to understand that God's love wasn't just universal, it was specifically for her.

We were talking outdoors, and the wind was blowing. I took a chance and told Nicole that the breeze was God's Spirit confirming how much he loved her. God was good to us that night—every time Nicole asked a question or seemed to be struggling, the breeze would pick up, as if to confirm that God was hearing her.

After about thirty minutes, the tears started flowing, really flowing. Years of pain, rejection, abuse, and bad decisions came pouring out. That was my cue to hand Nicole off to a female counselor, but not before praying with her. As we bowed our heads, and as Nicole prayed out loud and begged God to help her know his love, the wind just blew and blew, harder than it had all night. I just love it when God does that.

Pray that your daughter will know she is infinitely valuable to God. Pray that she'll look to God—not guys, stuff, money, popularity, sex, or anything else—for her source of unconditional love. Pray that she'll know that her value rests in her eternally created soul, not in how people see her. Pray Psalm 139:17–18 for her: *Lord God, I pray that my daughter will know that you think about her all the time. Let her understand that your thoughts about her outnumber the sand, and that even while she sleeps, you are with her and watching over her.*

### Pray that your daughter will be married to Jesus.

I'm encouraged to tell you that godly young girls and women aren't hard to find. In the acknowledgments, I listed several young women who inspired me while writing this chapter. They are living proof that girls don't have to cut corners in their relationship with Jesus in order to be accepted. And there are young women all over the world who feel quite comfortable in their relationship with Christ—so comfortable, in fact, that they're very selective about whom they're willing to date. My wife, Susie, was one of those young women.

When I met Susie, she was sixteen years old and a sophomore in high school. She was one of the most beautiful, godliest girls I'd ever met. And somehow I knew that those two things were related. I was attracted to Susie because she seemed so in love with Jesus. I knew that she would dump me in an instant (she did on several occasions) if I didn't meet her and Jesus's standards. Susie's love for Christ made me want to be a better Christian.

How does a young woman learn to be that content with who she is? How can our girls learn to trust Jesus completely and never compromise their walk with him? There's no doubt we have to teach and disciple them. We also have to love them unconditionally and provide a healthy family environment for them. But beyond those things, we want God to do a supernatural work in their hearts. We want God to woo them to himself.

In Hosea 2, God compared his relationship with Israel to that of a husband trying to woo back an unfaithful wife. He promised to speak kindly to her, to give her beautiful gifts, and then to betroth her to himself in righteousness, faithfulness, love, justice, and compassion (see vv. 14–23). In John 4, Jesus told an adulterous woman with five failed marriages that if she would learn to drink from his springs of living water, she would never thirst again (see vv. 7–26). And in Matthew 11, Jesus invited all who were weary from trying to always measure up to impossible standards to come to him, and he would give them rest (see vv. 28–30).

I can't think of any better prayers to pray for my girls. I want God to woo them; I want them to be completely satisfied with Jesus; and I want them to be free from the tyranny of having to look, act, weigh, dress, talk, and live a certain way to be accepted. In short, I want my girls to find their contentment, competency, and joy in Jesus. I want them to be married to him.

> For the last couple of years one theme I've shared with and prayed for my daughter has been Proverbs 4:23: "Above all else, guard your heart, for it is the wellspring of life." I've encouraged her to use this as a foundational verse for her life. When she was sixteen, I gave her a ring that I had given to her mother at about that age. It has a heart-shaped stone in it. It's a purity ring. When I gave it to her, I told her I was praying this verse for her.
>
> A praying dad

Pray that your daughter will find her life's joy and fulfillment in Christ. Pray that she'll hear and respond to the wooing and loving call of God in her life. Pray that she'll learn to grow her soul by feeding it daily in her relationship with Jesus. Pray that she will answer Jesus's call to come to him and that she will consider herself married to him. Pray that she will love and desire Jesus more than any other person or earthly treasure. Pray Proverbs 4:23 and Psalm 17:8 for your daughter: *Lord God, above all else, help my daughter to guard her heart, for it is the wellspring of life. Please keep her heart hidden safely in your love.*

### Pray that your daughter will know she is holy ground.

In Exodus 3, when Moses was confronted by God through the unlikely form of a burning bush, God instructed him, "Do not come any closer. . . . Take off your sandals, for the place where you are standing is holy ground" (v. 5). The theological implication of God's warning wasn't lost on Moses. Simply put, anyplace God is becomes holy—a desert bush, a temple, a tabernacle, or a human life. That's why one of the apostle Paul's favorite terms for the church was *saints*—literally, "holy ones." He knew what Moses had learned firsthand: when God moves into something, he makes it holy. That's especially true for people.

Unfortunately, too many Christians—specifically, Christian girls—fail to realize this. They live thinking they're too ordinary or too sinful for God to make them holy. Consider the following all-too-common, real-life example.

Kara is a young woman who attends our church. She recently discovered that her husband of only a few years had been living a double life. As she uncovered his infidelity and duplicity, her world caved in. The love of her life was gone. She had to find a job and begin rebuilding her new life—one that she had neither wanted nor chosen.

After a recent service at our church, Kara stayed for prayer. Her pain had caught up with her. The lies of Satan and the massive rejection she felt were getting the best of her. She just cried and cried. When I asked her what she was feeling, all she could muster through her tears was a weak, "I'm tired of not feeling special."

Anger boiled up inside of me. I wanted to curse Satan and rebuke the man who had done this to her. One man's sins, lies, and bad choices had convinced this Christian young woman that she was getting what she deserved, that this was all her fault, that she wasn't special. The implied lie was obvious: if she had been prettier, sweeter, sexier—whatever—none of this would have happened; her husband would still be there.

Nothing could be further from the truth. But Satan has never been interested in or felt restricted by truth. He just lies. We have to speak truth and shed light where he tries to insert darkness.

On this night, I broke into prayer. I prayed everything that we've been talking about in this chapter. I prayed that Kara would know that she is fearfully and wonderfully made. I prayed that she would love herself. I asked God to reveal himself to her as her husband, her Father, and her best friend. Then I added another prayer for Kara, one that I have prayed on countless occasions for my girls. I prayed that Kara would know she is holy ground.

Pray the same for your daughter. Pray that she'll know she is holy because God's Spirit lives in her. Pray that she'll know the miraculous power of God's transforming grace and that she is pure and righteous before God. Pray Exodus 3:5 for her: *Lord, please inhabit my daughter's life. Help her to know that because you are in her, she is holy ground.*

## A Verse to Pray for Your Daughter

Ephesians 2:10: *Lord Jesus, teach my daughter that she is your workmanship, created by you and for you to do good works that honor your name.*

# 9

# THEIR PLACE IN THIS WORLD

## PRAYING FOR YOUR CHILD'S MISSION

I N 1990, LEGENDARY singer and songwriter Michael W. Smith collaborated with songwriter Wayne Kirkpatrick to pen a song that struck a chord with countless young people in the United States and around the world. The song was released on Smith's album *Go West Young Man* and was entitled "Place in This World." It reflected the heart of a young person looking for his or her ultimate meaning, mission, and purpose in life.

One of the things that helped me want to turn my life back to Christ when I was a teenager was the sense of mission that accompanies the gospel. For a young man looking for a cause larger than himself, the kingdom of Jesus was an alluring option.

As we pray for our kids, we need to pray that they will have a sense of calling and personal mission. Heaven knows that this current generation of kids needs one.

### Generation Me

Our children could use a good dose of mission and others-centered orientation. They're part of a culture that constantly tells them that life is all about them. In her intriguing book *Generation Me: Why Today's Young Americans Are More Confident, Assertive, Entitled—and More Miserable Than Ever Before*, Jean Twenge argues that narcissism—the unhealthy focus on and prioritization of oneself—in American youth has hit an all-time high. Twenge, an associate professor of psychology at San Diego State University, compared data collected from 1.3 million youth over the last twenty-five years and determined that Americans born since 1974 have higher levels of self-centeredness and a "what's in it for me" mind-set. This caused her to label the group "Generation Me." Not surprisingly, Twenge doesn't think the trend is a good one. She links narcissistic thinking to a decreased value of personal relationships and higher levels of depression and anxiety in young people.[1]

The good news is that such me-centeredness isn't difficult to combat, especially if the young person is a Christ-follower. With the Holy Spirit already whispering to young Christians that Jesus, not themselves, is to be the center of their universe, and with the Bible repeatedly commanding them to consider others' needs before they consider their own, the shift from selfishness to selflessness can usually be brought about with pinpoint praying and good discipleship.

How do we pray for our children to discover their God-given mission and not focus on themselves? Let's learn from the Scriptures.


### A Big, Hairy, Audacious Vision

King David, arguably the greatest leader in Israel's history, had a vision to build a house for God. He longed to build a temple that would be an appropriate resting place for the ark of the covenant. He wanted the temple to state clearly to the rest of the nations that there was only one true God—the God of

Israel, the God who made the heavens. While David's vision was affirmed by the prophet Nathan, he also learned that it would be his son Solomon who would actually oversee the completion of the temple's construction and the fulfillment of David's vision. The Lord promised David, "When your days are over and you go to be with your fathers, I will raise up your offspring to succeed you, one of your own sons, and I will establish his kingdom. He is the one who will build a house for me, and I will establish his throne forever" (1 Chron. 17:11–12). David received a clear vision of the mission God had for his child, and he knew that he had to steward that vision well.

So do we. We may not know specifically what our kids will do. God probably won't tell us if our kids are to be missionaries or stay-at-home moms or teachers or painters. That's not for us to know. But we do know that God wants them to be kingdom builders. He wants them to give and serve and worship. He wants them to love his Word and hate sin. He wants them to manifest the fruit of his Spirit and help to spread his message around the world. God has a specific calling, mission, and vision for their lives, and it's our job as godly parents to help our kids discover it.

So what did David do? When told that his son was to build a house for God, how did David respond? He prayed. Specifically, he prayed back to God what God had promised him. He basically said, "Father, because you promised you would, I now have the boldness to ask you to continue my kingdom's reign through my son and to use him to build your house."

Let's hear it in David's own words: "And now, LORD, let the promise you have made concerning your servant and his house be established forever. Do as you promised" (1 Chron. 17:23). Isn't that amazingly simple? David prayed what God had promised. This is a classic example of true pinpoint praying in Scripture. David's prayer was specific, and it was based on God's Word to him. No wonder he prayed with such boldness. He was asking God to do what he'd already said he would.

The Bible is filled with truths about what God wants to do in the lives of his followers, including your child. You probably have many specific promises he has given you for your kid from his Word. (If not, you'll have them soon as you begin searching the Bible for pinpoint prayers for your kid.) So what do you do now? Start praying. Boldly go before God and pray his promises back to him. Tell him you believe that he has said he would do certain things in your child's life, and that's why you're asking him now.

For instance, suppose God leads you to pray Psalm 27:8 for your child: "My heart says of you, 'Seek his face!' Your face, LORD, I will seek." You feel that God wants you to pray regularly for your child to have a heart that seeks him more than anything else. So you do. You come before God regularly and remind him of what he's promised. You pray, "God, you said you wanted my child to have a heart that seeks after you. You said that was your will for his life. So, Father, based on your promise to me about my child, I'm asking you to keep your word. I'm asking you to give him a heart that seeks you more than anything or anyone else."

Such praying is exactly the kind of praying that David did; it's the kind of praying that the Bible encourages; and it's the kind of praying that God honors. If you believe that God has given you certain promises for your child, then you need to steward those promises by praying them back to him.

After David prayed that God would keep his promise concerning Solomon, he made sure that Solomon knew what God had promised. In other words, David told Solomon what God had planned for him to do: "Then he called for his son Solomon and charged him to build a house for the LORD, the God of Israel. . . . 'Now, my son, the LORD

110

be with you, and may you have success and build the house of the LORD your God, as he said you would'" (1 Chron. 22:6, 11).

We have an equal responsibility to teach our kids the vision that we know God has for them. A word of warning: Parents, be careful here. Don't impose your vision and will for your kid's life on God. You can teach with certainty the kind of kingdom citizen and mature follower that you know God wants your kid to be. That's a vision you can pass on with confidence. But you'll need to leave the details to God.

I could tell Will that I want him to be the next pastor of the church that I started. I could tell Emily that she is supposed to find the cure for cancer and AIDS. I could tell Sara that she is supposed to set a record for three-point shots in the WNBA. Those might be my desires for them, but I can't be sure they're God's.

> For years, I've prayed my son would have a heart for God. Now he leads worship in front of several hundred kids, even pulling teenage musicians together to form multiple bands. He's grown so much this past year that he now inspires my own faith.
>
> A praying dad

Teach your kid to seek God's mission and vision for his life. Pray that he'll know God's will, and support him as he pursues it. But don't tell him that you know specifically what God has for him. Even if you think you do, keep it to yourself and pray like crazy. He needs to hear it from God, not you.

So what happened with Solomon and the temple? God told David that Solomon would build the temple. David prayed that promise to God and shared it with Solomon. How did it end? Did Solomon complete David's vision and obey God by building the temple? The Bible tells us that at the dedication of the temple, Solomon reminded the people of his father's legacy and God's faithfulness:

My father David had it in his heart to build a temple for the Name of the LORD, the God of Israel. But the LORD said to my father David, "Because it was in your heart to build a temple for my Name, you did well to have this in your heart. Nevertheless, you are not the one to build the temple, but your son, who is your own flesh and blood—he is the one who will build the temple for my Name." The LORD has kept the promise he made. I have succeeded David my father and now I sit on the throne of Israel, just as the LORD promised, and I have built the temple for the Name of the LORD, the God of Israel.

2 Chronicles 6:7–10

God did as he promised.

Those verses give me great courage to keep praying for my kids and to never stop encouraging them to seek God's vision for their lives. As a praying parent, you need to know that God is as interested in keeping his promises for your child as he was for Solomon. God's call and mission for your child's life is no less significant. Don't ever stop praying for him and teaching him to pursue and obey God's mission.

### *Pray that your child will know her God-given role.*

Michael W. Smith's moving lyrics make good fodder for a pinpoint prayer for your child. There is a biblical character who actually modeled the type of confidence and certainty about his role on earth that Smith sang about.

In John 1, the writer tells us that John the Baptist was attracting a lot of attention. There hadn't been a prophetic voice on the religious landscape of Israel since Malachi—a dark period lasting four hundred years. Then John the Baptist burst on the scene, calling for repentance and declaring the kingdom of God. He became very popular and had quite a large following. There was much speculation about whether John was the promised Messiah.

When the Pharisees and other religious authorities came to investigate if John the Baptist was indeed the Christ, he gave a very direct answer: "He did not fail to confess, but confessed freely, 'I am not the Christ'" (John 1:20). John the Baptist had no delusions of grandeur. Don't miss the significance of his confession. Had he wanted to, he could have created a massive movement by claiming to be the Messiah. He could have grabbed instant fame and popularity if his ego had gotten the best of him.

But John knew his mission and what his role was. When pressed by the religious leaders to tell them his mission, he responded by quoting the prophet Isaiah: "I am the voice of one calling in the desert, 'Make straight the way for the Lord'" (v. 23). Seven hundred years earlier, Isaiah had predicted that the Christ would be preceded by a forerunner. He said that one would speak into the spiritual wilderness and darkness of Israel and call the people to get their hearts and lives ready for their coming king (see Isa. 40:1–11). John was raised knowing Isaiah's prophecies, and somewhere along the way, God led him to understand that Isaiah was talking about him.

Wouldn't it be wonderful if your kid could point to specific verses in the Bible that she knew were hers? I have a few passages that I go back to over and over again when I need to be reminded of why I am here. I know they weren't written about me specifically, but the Holy Spirit has pointed them out as being particularly representative of what he wants to accomplish in me.

Pray that your kid will have a clear sense of biblical direction and purpose for her life. Pray that God will write very specific biblical promises across her heart. Pray that she'll have hair-raising, tear-producing, vision-imparting, holy ambushes and inspirations from God through his Word. Then pray that she'll never stray from God's Word. Pray 2 Thessalonians 1:11

for your child: *Lord, please make my child worthy of your calling and equip her for every good work you have for her.*

### Pray that your child will love serving others.

It would be difficult to overstate the role that serving can play in the spiritual development of a young person. A kid who falls in love with serving will be better equipped to have meaningful relationships, to be a generous giver, to keep himself or herself in proper perspective, to pray more diligently, and to be more spiritually mature. That's why I pray every day that my kids will love to serve.

Serving is at the heart of a kingdom mind-set. Jesus himself could not have been more emphatic about the role that serving played in his kingdom. He said:

> Not so with you. Instead, whoever wants to become great among you must be your servant, and whoever wants to be first must be your slave.
>
> Matthew 20:26–27

> If anyone wants to be first, he must be the very last, and the servant of all.
>
> Mark 9:35

> For even the Son of Man did not come to be served, but to serve, and to give his life as a ransom for many.
>
> Mark 10:45

> But you are not to be like that. Instead, the greatest among you should be like the youngest, and the one who rules like the one who serves.
>
> Luke 22:26

The apostle Paul was equally emphatic. He wrote, "Do nothing out of selfish ambition or vain conceit, but in humility consider others better than yourselves. Each of you should look not only to your own interests, but also to the interests of others. Your attitude should be the same as that of Christ Jesus" (Phil. 2:3–5).

In the rank and order of God's kingdom, self comes last; others come first. In the economy of our culture, self rules everything. We need to pray that our kids won't fall for the "me first" mind-set of culture. We need to pray and teach them the power of yielding, deferring, and washing others' feet.

Once again, the example we set for our kids will go a long way in helping them develop a servant's heart. As with other disciplines such as giving, praying, and worshiping, our kids need to know that serving is a normal part of following Christ. It's what believers do. Here are some great ways to model an others-centered mind-set for your child and to help him catch the serving bug:

- *Adopt an elderly neighbor or a single mom and serve him or her regularly.* Mow the elderly neighbor's yard or help with basic house repairs. Make a grocery run for the single mom or watch her kids for a day. Involving your kid will help him see the power and joy of serving.
- *Take short-term mission trips as a family.* Every year our church sends more than a hundred men, women, and children to Juarez, Mexico, over the Thanksgiving weekend. They work with a ministry called Hands of Luke to help feed a Thanksgiving meal to over twenty thousand homeless and impoverished people. It's a great way to introduce kids to the value of missions and the value of sacrificing your own comfort and plans for the benefit of others. We have several families who have been back for repeat Thanksgiving visits to Juarez. Look for opportunities to help your kid experience cross-cultural missions and to see poverty up close. It will change his

perspective on both other people's needs and his own possessions.

- *Teach serving in your everyday routine.* I try to be very strategic about this. Sometimes I'll do my children's chores for them, especially when they're sick or busy with homework. I frequently get up early and buy my wife a cup of McDonald's coffee. (Okay, I confess, I buy myself one as well.) Little acts of service can go a long way in a home, especially for helping kids to see that serving is normal Christian behavior. Find ways to teach and model serving in the little things.

- *Finally, of course, pray.* Pray that your kid will develop a servant's heart. Pray that he'll learn to naturally think of others before he thinks of himself. Pray Paul's lofty command to the Philippian church for your child: *Father, help my child to have the same attitude, the same servant's heart, that Jesus had.*

### In the Line of Fire

On July 10, 2001, twenty-three-year-old forest service firefighter Rebecca Welch, along with thirteen other firefighters, was part of a larger group battling a wicked blaze in Okanogan-Wenatchee National Forest in Washington State. The fire, now known as the Thirtymile Fire, spread from 5 to 2,100 acres in just two and a half hours and trapped nearly two dozen people in a narrow portion of the Chenoweth River canyon.

Firefighters are trained to always have an escape route, but on this day, poor decision making (criminal negligence charges were later filed against a forestry service supervisor) and the rapidly changing conditions of the fire left the firefighters stranded. When the group realized that they were trapped and would soon be overtaken by the flames, their field commander ordered them to deploy their emergency fire tents. Each tent resembles a pup tent, is made of a fire-retardant material designed to withstand temperatures up to six hundred degrees, and is meant to be used by only one person. Each firefighter carries a tent and has been trained in proper deployment techniques. Even with the protection of a tent, a firefighter's chances of surviving a fire in the wild aren't all that great. There are simply too many variables. The tents are designed as a last-ditch effort only.

As Rebecca Welch was hurriedly deploying her tent, she heard panicked screams coming from nearby. She then saw Bruce and Paula Hagemeher, both in their fifties, running toward her group. The Hagemehers had been hiking in the area and had also been trapped by the rapidly spreading flames. They had no protection and were moments away from being overtaken by the wall of fire. Welch quickly grabbed the frightened couple and threw them under her tent. She then jumped on top of them and tried to cover the three of them with her tent. She couldn't. While the Hagemehers were mostly protected, Welch remained dangerously exposed. The three of them used their hands to beat back flames and hold down the tent corners as the fire raged over them. They miraculously survived. When the fire finally passed, the Hagemehers suffered only from smoke inhalation. Rebecca Welch was treated for second-degree burns on one side of her body. Tragically, four of her fellow firefighters died in their tents.

Rebecca Welch received numerous awards and recognitions for her act of bravery, including being honored by Congress and being the youngest person ever to receive the Stihl National Forestry Heroism Award. Bruce and Paula Hagemeher know they are alive today because of Welch's heroism. Had she not acted as quickly and as selflessly as she did, there would have been at least two more deaths that day in the Chenoweth canyon.

Not only do I find Rebecca Welch's example to be inspiring, but she also modeled the kind of heart and others-first mentality that I am praying for my kids to have. The generation of Christ-followers we are parenting will be positioned in the line of fire between the kingdom of God and the domain of darkness. They will be fighting to hold back the onslaught of sin, moral relativism, and humanism that are so quickly embraced by many of their peers. And, most importantly, they will be fighting to save the souls of a generation that is precariously close to perishing in eternity. The stakes couldn't be any higher.

Too many Christian kids hit adulthood thinking that life is about making money and being happy. Few have ever done any serious thinking about their mission and purpose. Most can't name their spiritual gifts, and an equal number have an "it's all about me" mind-set.

But all hope is not lost. My inspiration for this chapter wasn't the kids who don't get it, but the kids who do. I am inspired by Shane, a high school football player who chose to spend a week in Mississippi helping with Katrina relief instead of playing in his team's season opener. The coaches weren't pleased with his decision, but Shane will never forget the time he spent rebuilding the hurricane-damaged home of an impoverished, elderly African American woman with a learning disability.

I am inspired by Hannah, a third grader who prayed for and ministered to her schoolmate whose father was dying of cancer. And Kimmie, a high school junior with aspirations of playing college basketball, found a whole new level of joy shooting hoops with a bunch of kids in an orphanage in Nicaragua. And Hudson, who delayed his first year of college so he could travel to China, where he spent the year translating the Scriptures into the Mandarin language and distributing them to persecuted believers. And David, a high school senior who leads nearly a hundred of his peers in worship each week. Finally, I am inspired by the children in our church, who recently took an impromptu offering in their class so they could help pay for a year of school for an orphan in Nicaragua.

These sweet kids, and countless others like them, tell me that "Generation Me" isn't the best name for the kids we're now raising. There are plenty who understand that the world doesn't revolve around them. They give and serve and defer to others on a regular basis. They're praying every day for God to show them their place in this world. And when God tells them what that is, they seize it with abandon. They're "Generation Others" because they seek to benefit others. They're "Generation Yes" because they're learning to say yes to God no matter what. And they're "Generation Impact" because through their obedience they are changing the world.

Pray for them. Even as you read this, the torch of leadership is passing from our generation to theirs. We must decrease; they must increase. As they become more prominent, our role moves to one of intercession. We need to pave the way for them through prayer. Pray that their hearts will always belong to God and that they will be tender and responsive to his leadings.

### A Verse to Pray for Your Child

2 Chronicles 16:9: *Father, your eyes roam to and fro throughout the earth, looking for those whose hearts are completely yours so you can strongly support them. Please help my child to have a passionate heart for you; please give her your strong support as she seeks to honor you.*

# PART 3

# PINPOINT PRAYERS FOR THOSE WHO WILL IMPACT YOUR CHILD'S LIFE

Follow my example, as I follow the example of Christ.

1 Corinthians 11:1

# 10

## FOLLOW ME

### PRAYING FOR YOUR CHILD'S ROLE MODELS

RECENTLY, WHILE TEACHING our church about the importance of training and praying for our children, I gave them a rather startling and troubling object lesson. I walked out onstage, leading a third grade child by a rope. Her hands were bound in front of her, and she looked the part of a captive little girl. The image immediately got the attention of everyone in the room. I then told our church, "I believe our kids are being stolen from us. I think they're being taken captive and led away. And the tragic part is, most of us are too busy, distracted, or spiritually undiscerning to even notice."

The most troubling thing about the scene I portrayed for our church is that it's biblical. It's one of the consequences that God says would come to his people if they ever strayed from him and started worshiping false gods. Not only would the consequences of their idolatry and rebelliousness affect them, but it would also terribly impact subsequent generations. Here

123

is Moses's synopsis of this nightmarish scene: "Your sons and daughters will be given to another nation, and you will wear out your eyes watching for them day after day, powerless to lift a hand" (Deut. 28:32).

I believe that our children are being taken captive and deported to a land not our own, and that this current generation of adults is too distracted and spiritually impotent to even realize it. "Who is the enemy?" you ask. "What nation is taking them captive?" Pick your *ism*: materialism, humanism, relativism, Darwinism, rationalism, atheism, syncretism—the list goes on and on. And as we saw in the last chapter, many believing adults today aren't spiritually mature enough to discern that anything is happening.

## Making a Good Impression

I'd like to introduce you to the most important person in your child's life—*you*. If you are married, then your mate shares an equal load in impacting your child. But *you* are the adult in your child's life whom you can control the most, and *you* can make sure you're serious about raising a godly, discipled kid. So put down this book, go look in a mirror, and tell yourself that you will not allow your child to grow up as a spiritual orphan. Commit today to make your life's mission raising discipled, spiritually mature kids.

In Deuteronomy 6, God gave a command through Moses to the nation of Israel that became a foundational verse for the Hebrew culture:

> Hear, O Israel: The LORD our God, the LORD is one. Love the LORD your God with all your heart and with all your soul and with all your strength. These commandments that I give you today are to be upon your hearts. Impress them on your

children. Talk about them when you sit at home and when you walk along the road, when you lie down and when you get up. Tie them as symbols on your hands and bind them on your foreheads. Write them on the doorframes of your houses and on your gates.

Deuteronomy 6:4–9

Notice that the command wasn't just to love the Lord wholly but to teach the next generation to do the same. God placed the responsibility of passing the spiritual torch of faith to the nation's children squarely on the shoulders of their parents. He left them absolutely no wiggle room. It wasn't up to the rabbi, the synagogue leader, or the high priest; parents were commanded to train their own children in matters of faith.

That command still stands today, and the need for us to obey it couldn't be any greater. When I began researching for this book, I asked the two very talented and capable staff members who lead my church's children's and student ministries for their input. I asked what they thought was the greatest need of children and youth today. They both gave the same answer, and they gave it with great conviction: kids today need parents who are committed to discipling them. They don't need parents who just make sure their kids are in good, discipling ministries, although that's certainly important. No, what they need is a mom and dad who are equally committed to raising spiritual giants.

Moses commanded the Hebrews to *impress* the teachings of God onto their kids (see Deut. 6:7). That's what discipling parents do—they make an impression. They do more than just talk; they model. Kids in disciple-making homes learn from their parents' example how to serve, give, pray, worship, repent, forgive and seek forgiveness, yield, and feed their souls through God's Word.

So, what are our kids learning from us? What values are we passing on to them? In a recent survey by the Pew Research Center, young people were asked, "What is your generation's most important goal?" Eighty percent responded, "Getting rich." Only 4 percent said, "Becoming more spiritual."[1] Is that mind-set not a reflection of the values we have taught and modeled for our kids? It appears that we've got some work (and praying) to do.

## Do Like I Do

You may have heard the phrase, "Do like I tell you, not like I do." It's a favorite escape clause for parents whose kids catch them trying to enforce a rule that they themselves don't keep. I can tell you exactly where I was when my dad first used it on me.

I was an eager fifteen-year-old with a new learner's permit. I was driving with my dad back into Austin from our lake house in his giant, four-door Buick. (We called it the Land Barge.) The trip took us down a curvy, hilly road—the perfect route for a novice driver to try out his skills. We came to a certain curve where I had seen my dad cut from the outside lane to the inside on at least a dozen occasions. I did exactly the same. Without signaling, I whipped the car down low in the curve and hugged the yellow stripe as tightly as I could. It was awesome! That is, until my dad grabbed the wheel and jerked the car back over to the slower, outside lane. When I told my dad that I had learned that cool maneuver from him . . . well, let's just say that it was a while before I was driving again. And I have to admit, I've quoted the "Do like I tell you, not like I do" line to my own son on many occasions.

So what would it take for you to be able to say to your child, "Hey, imitate me"? Instead of saying, "Do like I tell you, not like I do," when might you be able to say, "Do like I do"? In spiritual matters, you should always be ready to be an example and role model for your child. He shouldn't have to look elsewhere to find his spiritual heroes. He may have other spiritual mentors besides you, but his first example of true godliness ought to be right there at home.

The apostle Paul didn't hesitate to offer himself as an example to believers. In his first letter to the Christians in Corinth, Paul urged them to follow his example: "Therefore I urge you to imitate me" (1 Cor. 4:16). Later on, he repeated the command and added an explanation: "Follow my example, as I follow the example of Christ" (1 Cor. 11:1). In other words, "You'll be all right if you just watch me and do as I do. I'm looking closely at Jesus. Whatever he does, I'll do. So just keep your eyes on me, and you'll be fine."

I've had countless occasions on mountain trails and even dangerous mountain ledges where I've told my kids or other less experienced hikers to watch me and do exactly as I do. There's nothing arrogant or proud in my comments. Experience has taught me how to navigate certain types of terrain. I feel confident showing others how to do the same.

We ought to be equally confident spiritually. Our kids should be able to look at our lives and learn how to safely navigate life's most dangerous terrain. They will take their cues from us when it comes to relationships, money, forgiveness, sexuality, church participation, and our treatment of the poor, the elderly, and people of differing ethnicities. They'll notice when we pray and when we don't. They'll see us reading the Bible, or they'll note that we rarely do. They'll pick up on our serving habits, or they'll see that we rarely stop to serve others. But good or bad, our kids are watching. Are they learning how to be godly?

## Who, Me? A Mentor?

Now, some of you might be saying, "But wait a minute! I'm still a young Christian. How can I teach my child to be godly when I struggle with it every day?"

I'm so glad you asked. If you're feeling a bit behind the curve on this one, don't panic. It's never too late to start growing as a Christian. Go back and look at the chapters on praying specifically for your child. Every prayer I mentioned there, you can pray for yourself as well. Start praying that you'll love God's Word, that you'll hate sin, and that you'll love to worship. Try to read the Bible and pray at least a few minutes every day. I also strongly encourage you to join a Sunday school class or a small group in your church. You need other godly adults encouraging you as you develop spiritually.

You can start maturing as a Christ-follower today, but don't wait any longer! Your kid needs you to press on to maturity so she can follow your example.

## Planned Discipleship

Pray for God to show you how to be strategic about discipling your child. Pray that you'll have the wisdom to know when and how to build good, Christ-following principles into your child's life. Take to heart the teaching offered by Solomon to train your child in righteousness (see Prov. 22:6). Training isn't haphazard; pray for a plan.

Here are a few ways to build strategic discipleship into your parenting routine.

*Meals.* These most basic and regular of all family gatherings are great places to teach spiritual principles. At a recent family dinner, Susie shared with our girls about a difficult time she was having spiritually. Through tears she talked about her "dark night of the soul." She shared how she felt that God had stopped speaking to her over a year before. Christians throughout the centuries have experienced similar periods of silence. Susie had been reading about them and was able to share how and why God sometimes is present without speaking. It was an intensely beautiful conversation. I was proud to be married to a woman who could so powerfully prepare our girls for their own potential spiritual struggles.

Family meals are definitely times to laugh, catch up on each other's day, and enjoy small talk. But they're also great settings for discipleship. Take advantage of them. Strategically plan to use the dinner hour to talk about spiritual issues and practical principles for Christian living.

*Prayer.* Don't just pray *for* your kid, pray *with* him. Let your kid learn to pray by listening to your prayers. Again, use mealtimes to model good prayer habits. Let him hear you genuinely thank God for what he has provided. Also, pray over your child before he goes to sleep. Think about how natural prayer will feel to your child after he has been prayed over by you every night at bedtime. Make praying with your kid part of his nightly routine.

*Church attendance and serving.* If your kid goes to Sunday school, a youth program, or a church worship event with you, then she's probably hearing Bible teaching. Talk with her about what she's learning. Ask what her lesson was about and how it impacted her. Ask her what God wants her to do as a result of what she learned. Get her in the habit of listening to and then acting on the teaching of God's Word.

Also, try to worship and serve together as a family. Your kid will learn a lot just from sitting next to you in a church service. She'll hear you sing, watch you take notes, and hear you say "Amen" to a prayer or a profound teaching point. She'll also learn by watching you mow an elderly neighbor's yard or play with a group of kids in a shelter or orphanage.

Use your worship and service as times to impart good spiritual values to your kid.

*Transitional moments.* If you plan ahead, you can build discipleship into key events in your child's life. His first day of school, his sixteenth birthday, his first solo drive in a car, his first job, an A or an F on his exam, or his high school graduation are all opportunities to teach biblical principles to your child. Stay alert and ask God to help you plan to mark critical transitions in your child's life with appropriate levels of teaching, affirmation, and prayer.

When my son turned thirteen, I invited all the men in our family to meet at our house for lunch with him. Afterward we sat around the table and took turns talking to him about what it meant to be a Christian man. It was an incredibly powerful moment as his grandfathers, uncles, and cousins shared what God had taught them over the years. My son requested a similar type of gathering for his eighteenth birthday. We did similar luncheon events with the women in our family and my daughters when they each turned thirteen.

Pray for God to help you develop a good discipleship strategy for your kids. Pray that their spiritual training wouldn't be an afterthought or a low priority. Ask God to make you an effective discipler of your children.

## Unplanned Discipleship

For every planned opportunity that parents have to strategically teach their kids about spiritual matters, there are infinitely more unplanned opportunities that will arise in the daily routine of life. Pray that God will speak to your spirit and alert you to teachable moments as they pop up. Sometimes your unplanned, unscripted responses to life can impact your child more than your planned and controlled teaching sessions. When you encounter a homeless man on the corner, when a rude driver cuts you off in traffic, when your credit card is refused at the grocery store, when your neighbor's dog trashes your garden for the third time, when you and your spouse are having a tense financial discussion, when your family's twelve-year-old black Lab has to be put down, when your body starts becoming less dependable as you grow older—each of these is a wonderful opportunity for you to model God's grace and biblical principles for your kids.

My friend Nancy buried her husband a few years ago. He was a godly man who died after a two-year battle with cancer. Nancy now raises their two kids alone, acting as both mother and father to them. She's also their primary example of what a Christ-follower looks like. I asked Nancy to write about how she modeled faith for her kids.

The kids and I were planning a trip to Six Flags Fiesta Texas in San Antonio for a fun-filled day last summer. We were all ready to go, towels and sunscreen in hand, when one of them asked if I had our season passes. I looked for them in my "Fun Things to Do" file, where I knew I had put them last. Of course they were not there. Panic set in as we all three realized that we might not be going after all. After ransacking the whole house and coming up empty-handed, my eleven-year-old son said, "Mom, let's pray about it." After all, he had seen that work for me many times before. I often pray for God to help me find the latest thing I've misplaced, and he has come through every time. So the three of us held hands and prayed.

As I took a deep breath and began the next phase of the search, I knew my faith was being tested. I realized there was a lot more at stake than just my kids' disappointment. What if I did not find the passes? How would that affect my kids spiritually? Did I trust God to help me with something so minor? A peace came over me just as the thought came into my head to look in the car. I looked under the driver's seat, where I know I had looked before, and there they were: Fiesta Texas season passes. I ran inside waving the tickets, and we all rejoiced and thanked God. God does care about the big and little things in our lives. I'm grateful he showed himself real to us in answering our prayer!

Do you have the courage to step out in faith in front of your kids? Are you willing to let them watch you struggle—try, succeed, and even fail—in your faith? Remember, your kids aren't expecting a perfect faith, just an authentic one. Ask God to help you take advantage of the unplanned discipleship moments in your lives. Your kids will be better for it.

## Pray for Godly Role Models

Before we conclude this chapter, we need to talk about the other people in our kids' lives who will influence them. Any wise and godly parent knows that we cannot always be physically present with our kids. There will be times when we simply cannot be there to parent them. For those times, we need to pray for the other people—kids and adults—who will impact our kids.

When I was only thirteen, I entered into a three-year, very serious season of rebellion. I don't blame anyone but myself—my spiritual immaturity and my many poor choices—for this sad period in my life. I was a wild and unruly kid. I strayed from what I knew was right and started living a very out-of-control, sometimes dangerous lifestyle.

One of the key factors in my rebellion was my choice of role models. I had stopped going to church and therefore lost contact with some of the godly people in my life. I was also a competitive water-skier, and most of the people I trained with were not good influences on me. I was a thirteen-year-old kid skiing and hanging out with some of the greatest skiers in the world, and I was totally in awe of them. I completely adopted their way of talking, acting, and thinking. I don't blame them; they were simply lost people acting lost. But it wasn't a pretty picture.

Then—and I'm quite sure that my mother's prayers had something to do with this—I stepped in a hole in my backyard one summer and seriously injured my ankle. My skiing days, at least for that summer, were over. And that's the year I got reacquainted with some of the godly people at my church. I eventually started attending again, got ambushed by God, and have never looked back. God changed my role models and my peer group—and my life.

You can't always be with your kid. He or she is going to have coaches, teachers, tutors, and scout leaders, as well as friends and their parents, who will be with him or her at times when you're not. Pray for those people. Pray that God will surround your child with men, women, and other kids who love God. Pray that your child will have great role models in the sports, school subjects, and hobbies he or she is interested in.

The example of Paul's relationship with young Timothy encourages me to pray for my kids. Timothy grew up in a spiritually divided home. Both his mother and grandmother followed Christ, but his father was an unbeliever. God put Timothy on Paul's radar, and the saintly apostle adopted the young man as his spiritual son (see 1 Tim. 1:2).

I want God to do that for my kids. I want him to surround them with godly people—men, women, and even friends— who will pour into them, pray for them, and encourage them to stay on the high road when I'm not around. I want God to give them each a godly, Paul-like person who can help to teach and train them.

As your kid grows older and becomes more independent, he or she is going to have more freedom to choose friends and to be influenced by the thinking and values of other adults. Pray that God will bless your son or daughter with a long line of spiritual heroes who will supplement and support what you are working for and praying for him or her to become. Pray that your Timothy will be adopted by a Paul.

Here are some summary suggestions for creating pinpoint prayers for your child's role models:

- *Pray for his friends.* Ask God to give your kid godly, Christian peers. Pray that his friends will help him make good choices and stay out of trouble.
- *Pray for her teachers.* Pray that God will bring godly teachers and school counselors into your child's life. Pray that your kid will connect with godly, believing teachers on her campus.
- *Pray for his coaches.* Next to parents, coaches may spend more time with and have more impact on kids than any other adult. Coaches can have a significant lasting impact on children—for good or for bad. Pray that your child will be blessed with godly coaches. Pray that the adults who coach him will be as interested in teaching character development, good team principles, and the importance of hard work, self-discipline, and training as they are in winning.
- *Pray for her friends' parents.* Pray for God to lead your kid into homes where the parents are as godly and as committed to Christ as you are. Pray that he will protect your child from any unhealthy lifestyles and behaviors her friends' parents may have.
- *Pray for godly mentors.* I was blessed to have godly men take interest in me in my high school years. Later on

God provided equally godly men to mentor me in my early and very formative years in ministry. Pray the same for your child. Ask God to bring godly pastors, children and youth ministers, Sunday school teachers, and church leaders into your child's life. Pray that he will have countless up-close examples of godly men and women who love God and who live Christ-honoring lives.

> I pray for my children's friends, mentors, and other adults who might be influential people in their lives (some of whom I may never know, see, or be aware of). I pray for their teachers—their energy, ideas, compassion, health, desire, wisdom, leadership, and knowledge.
>
> A praying mom

## A Verse to Pray for Your Child

Psalm 141:5: *Father, please surround my child with righteous friends who will speak truth to her and rebuke her when she's wrong.*

# *11*

# THE MOST CRITICAL MOMENT IN PARENTING

I'LL NEVER FORGET that day in the park. My son, Will, was about three. I was playing with him at a playground near our house. He was laughing and giggling, and then he gave me this piercing look. It was like time just froze in that instant. I can still see his face. In the moment that Will looked at me, I saw him as an adult, not a child. I saw him as a man. It was like God was saying to me, "Will is not yours; he's mine. I have plans for him that you know nothing about. I will care for him and protect him, but I need you to let go of him."

Those were some tough words for a dad to hear. I didn't like them. But I got the message. I made a clear decision to start preparing my son for the day that he would leave Susie's and my care (a day that arrived in August 2005). I began looking for opportunities to grow and stretch him. I began to be more aware of teachable moments and of his critical life transitions. When I crossed that emotional line, I became a better parent. When you cross that same line, you will become a better parent too.

Have you had that encounter with God when he gently reminded you of his claim on your child's life? Maybe it came when you were rocking her to sleep one night in her nursery, or when he took his first steps. Maybe God spoke to you when she said her first words. Or maybe you saw it when you dropped him off for his first day of school. Whatever the occasion, I bet you've had that moment when God reminded you of your job description as a parent. If you haven't had that moment yet, start praying for it. You won't love your kid any less, but you will see him or her differently.

## Letting Go

Parenting is the only God-designed relationship where the goal is separation. Parents succeed when their offspring make a complete break from dependence upon them and move on to live healthy, independent lives of their own. If we parent well, the day will come when our children can function well without our ongoing oversight.

Nothing could go more against our parenting instincts. Everything in us wants to continue to protect, guide, teach, and even correct our children. But as they grow older and more mature, they are supposed to lean on us less and less. Our greatest parenting moment comes when our kids walk out into the world, fully equipped to function as God-honoring, independent young adults, without us looking over their shoulders. As parents, we need to be working toward that day. More importantly, we need to be praying for it. Our children's lives are going to be filled with countless firsts and new levels of independence. Let's start praying for them now.

138

## A Baby, a Basket, and a River

Baby Moses was born into the hostile environment of a people enslaved in a brutal and ruthless nation. At the time of his birth, Egyptian soldiers had standing orders to kill all Hebrew male infants in an effort to help control the surging Hebrew population. Imagine the terrible mixed emotions and fears Moses's mother must have felt as she saw that God had graced her with a beautiful new baby boy. She could tell instantly that he was special. She also knew that he probably wouldn't live to see his first birthday.

Moses's parents did their best to keep his birth a secret. They, along with Moses's sister, Miriam, tried to hide him from the ever-watching eyes of the Egyptian soldiers. Have you ever tried to hide a two-month-old? They don't hide well. They gurgle and coo and cry. We can only imagine the terror-filled moments Moses's family must have faced as they tried desperately to hush their sweet baby while the soldiers lurked outside, making their murderous rounds. At three months, Moses was too big to hide. The family could no longer keep his presence a secret from the soldiers.

The text of Exodus doesn't offer us many details about the decision that Moses's parents faced. We can be sure that it was gut-wrenching, for they determined that placing the baby in a basket and leaving him along the shore of the Nile River was their *best* option. The Scriptures simply read, "Now a man of the house of Levi married a Levite woman, and she became pregnant and gave birth to a son. When she saw that he was a fine child, she hid him for three months. But when she could hide him no longer, she got a papyrus basket for him and coated it with tar and pitch. Then she placed the child in it and put it among the reeds along the bank of the Nile. His sister stood at a distance to see what would happen to him" (Exod. 2:1–4).

Moses's parents let go of their baby, literally. They had no choice. If he'd remained with them, he would have most certainly been killed. They couldn't flee with him, and they couldn't give him away. Abandoning him—trusting him to the mercy of God—was all they could do. But what they didn't know was that releasing Moses wasn't just their only option, it was part of God's plan.

## A Defining Moment

Moses's parents' decision to let go of their son turned out to be a defining moment in history. You probably know the story. Pharaoh's daughter discovered the basket, instantly took to the handsome baby, and decided she wanted to keep him. Moses's quick-thinking sister, who was watching from the riverbank nearby, told the Egyptian princess that she just happened to know a young Hebrew woman who would be happy to nurse the baby. By the end of the day, Moses's parents had their baby back, this time with the legal protection of Pharaoh's household.

But God still wasn't done working. He had plans that neither Moses's parents nor the young Egyptian princess knew about. Pharaoh's daughter had unwittingly brought the future liberator of the Hebrew nation into her father's house. God needed Moses to be well trained, educated, and very familiar with the ways of Egyptian life. His experiences growing up in Pharaoh's house would prepare him not just to serve as Israel's rescuer but also to serve as her leader after they were free. When Moses's parents left him by the riverside, they started a series of events that would end up changing history.

Knowing when and how to let go of our children is that important. They can't become the people that God intends if we don't get out of the way. Start praying today for your parenting to produce healthy, mature, independent adults.

## "Who Is Willing to, Uh, Share This Woman?"

I've performed more wedding ceremonies than I can remember. I've seen it all—fainting brides, inebriated in-laws, missing grooms, runaway flower girls, bumbled vows, forgotten song lyrics, and misplaced rings, wedding licenses, bouquets, boutonnieres, and wedding veils. Yep, I've seen it all. Or at least I thought I had, until I met Momzilla. She pushed my wedding experience to a whole new level.

I was marrying a sweet young couple just out of college. They were godly, committed to Christ and each other, and very serious about having a great marriage. We had done several sessions of premarital counseling together. They had started praying together and were taking the high road. I felt pretty good about their chances. Until I met Momzilla. Unfortunately, I met her way too late.

It was just before the wedding ceremony. The couple had agreed to meet beforehand to take pictures with their families. When I arrived at the church, the bride immediately introduced me to her mom. Then Momzilla grabbed me by the arm in a deathlike grip and quickly pulled me over to the side of the room. She looked me in the eye and said something like, "Look, preacher, I don't know what you do or say at other weddings, but this one is different. When my husband walks our daughter down the aisle, you will *not* ask the 'Who gives this woman to this man' question. You won't say anything about giving anybody away. Find something nice and polite to say, but you won't even mention us giving away our daughter. 'Cause we're not. We'll share her. We'll welcome that boy [the groom] into our family. But we are *not* giving her away. Got it?"

Being the independent, brave, you're-not-going-to-push-this-preacher-around kind of guy that I am, I did exactly as I was told. I mumbled some weak, "Who welcomes this man into their family?" (I should have said *"dysfunctional* family.") I have no doubt that if I hadn't, Momzilla would have stood up during the ceremony and corrected me.

Maybe you're thinking, *I know I'm not that bad. I'd never do that to my child. Sure, sure, I know I'll have to let go some-day. I know that. But my family isn't living as slaves in Egypt. No one is trying to take my children. My kids are very young. I've got years before I need to think about letting go.* Actually, you don't.

As godly parents, we need to come to grips with a time-less biblical reality: our kids are not our own. They're God's. God gives us children to raise, love, teach, and train for his glory. But like everything else we have, they're on loan. We are stewards of our children; we are not their owners. I'm asking you to consider—and more importantly, to pray about—accepting the fact that you are raising kids who are not really yours, kids whom you are training and preparing to leave home. I want you to begin to pray about, prepare for, and parent toward the day when your children make a clean, healthy, and God-honoring break from their depen-dence on you.

## The Benefits of Letting Go

As with every area of obedience, there are several benefits to obeying God as a parent and preparing your child for a healthy separation from you. Here are just a few of them.

### You will parent more strategically.

It's easy to slip into the rut of coexistence with our kids and forget that we really have a job to do as parents. Busyness and our rush-around lifestyles often make us less effective at teaching our kids what they need to know before they move out on their own. But as you embrace the concept of parenting for good separation, you will begin to think differently. Your priorities will change. You will begin to see and pray for opportunities to train up your child in the way he should go (see Prov. 22:6).

For instance, I have some friends who pay their bills online. Each month they sit down with their ninth grade daughter and involve her in the process. She sees where all their money goes and how much they have. But most importantly, she sees that the first several payments go to their church and other ministries they support. By parenting strategically, that couple is not only showing their daughter how to be financially responsible, they're teaching her the value of financial stewardship.

### You will grow up.

Too many of us live vicariously through our children. A kid's first grade project becomes our project and ends up looking more like a boardroom presentation than a first grader's work. Others of us didn't separate well from our own parents and don't really want our kids to separate from us. But when you begin praying about your role as coach and equipper in your child's life, you will have to mature. God will show you your own weaknesses and immature areas and push you to grow out of them. God's Spirit will grow you so you can better grow your kid.

### Your child will mature more quickly.

I was raised in the home of an elected official. My dad held local, state, and even national public offices before I graduated from high school. Through my dad's travels, responsibilities, and many awards, I was privileged to meet people from all walks of life, including some very powerful people. Those experiences taught me how to handle myself around adults. Beyond that, Dad was always willing to talk about the joys and struggles of his public life, which helped me grow. I gained a perspective on the world that I wouldn't have had if Dad had sheltered me from the rough-and-tumble world of politics. Giving your child opportunities and exposing him to your world will help him mature.

If you're spiritually alert, you can use your own experiences to give your kid a biblical perspective on life. I can't count the number of conversations Susie or I have had with our kids about biblical truths while simply reflecting on the events— good or bad—in the lives of those around us. When the 9/11 attacks happened, our girls were still young. The news coverage obviously scared and confused them. It gave us the chance to talk to them about sin, evil, and God's mercy and forgiveness. Other times we just talk to them about what's happening in their friends' lives—one friend's parents are divorcing, another's dad has cancer, and another got caught cheating on a test. If you stay alert to what's going on, God will provide you with countless opportunities to teach your kid and to help him learn to look at the world through a biblical lens. Having a biblical worldview is a major step in your child's preparation to enter adulthood as a healthy and secure Christ-follower.

### You will prepare your child for life's tests.

I remember talking to a parent who, along with her husband, had just made the difficult decision to move their eighth grader from a private to a public school when she started ninth grade. The reasons for the change were many, but the primary one was about exposure. The parents simply wanted their daughter to get a taste of the real world while she was still under their roof. They figured they had a better chance of setting their daughter up to make good choices later in life if they were able to guide her through similar choices while she was still young.

You can't always protect your child from the spiritual realities of the world he lives in. God doesn't keep us from being tempted but rather equips us with his Spirit so we can overcome in the face of temptation (see Matt. 4:1–11 and 1 Cor. 10:13). Parent and pray with the same goal for your child. Pray that you'll have the wisdom to know when to let your child face certain tests in life—when to let her start dating, when to let him take a road trip with his friends, when to let her stay alone in the house, when to get him a bank account. Such opportunities also include temptations, some of which you'll want your child to face *before* he is out of your care. Pray that you'll establish just the right balance between parental oversight and your child's choices. Pray that you can effectively guide your child through important tests before he has to face them on his own.

### Your faith will grow.

Every form of stewardship increases faith—stewarding money, resources, time, and talents. Stewarding your child is no exception. As you pray and see God come through for her, your faith will grow. Moses's parents must have marveled at God's plan when they not only received their son back from the river but also realized that God had provided the protection and education for him that they never could have. God always does more with something when you release it. As you pray for the faith to release your child to God, you will see him do things in and through her that you could have never orchestrated on your own. That will increase your faith and hers.

### You will look to God for your child's protection.

We talked in an earlier chapter about praying for our kids' protection. It's easy to forget who is ultimately responsible for their safety. We forget Jesus's great promise in Matthew 18:10: "See that you do not look down on one of these little ones. For I tell you that their angels in heaven always see the face of my Father in heaven." In other words, "Don't you ever mess with a kid! They always have angels in the presence of God watching over them." We forget that God is really the one protecting our children.

But as our kids get older and become more independent, we are reminded of just how little control we have over what happens in their lives. We *can't* always protect them. That's when prayer and faith kick in. Can you imagine what Moses's mother prayed when she left that basket on the bank of the Nile? *O God, I can't protect this child. I can't keep him safe. I yield him to you. Would you please watch over and protect him? Would you please govern his life? We've done everything we can for him. Now he's in your hands.*

God was her only hope, and he was Moses's only hope, and that's exactly how God wanted it. As parents, we need to be as careful and vigilant as possible in protecting our children. That's part of our God-given stewardship of their lives. But ultimately, their

> Lord, protect my children from the enemy, who sows distrust, anger, and pride in their hearts. Help them to learn the lessons you would have for them so that they may not stumble and fall. May their hearts be filled by your Holy Spirit so that they would gain insight, wisdom, and knowledge of you. Cover them with your glory and turn them into mighty warriors for your kingdom, and please give me the courage to allow them to be who you have called them to be.
>
> A praying dad

safety, health, and prosperity are his concern. If you're going to have the courage to walk through the stages of letting go of your children—her first time with a babysitter, his first day of school, her first time to spend the night with friends, his first solo drive in the car, her first date, and so on—then you have to know and believe that God will look out for them. Pray for the faith to ultimately trust your child's safety and future to God. Moses's mother didn't have a choice. She had to trust God with her child. So must we.

### *You will see your child through God's eyes, not just your own.*

I seriously doubt that Moses's parents looked at that bundle in the basket and saw the future deliverer of Israel. They knew their son was special, but probably not *that* special. Few of us ever start off by looking at our children's skills, talents, and passions through God's eyes. We look at our kids and see presidents, CEOs, business owners, doctors, and very successful people. We see them living happy, prosperous, and comfortable lives. But like Moses's parents, we probably don't see the plan God has for them.

As you pray for God's will for your child's life, you will begin to see her true kingdom potential. You will begin to warm up to the idea that God's plan for her may be radically different than your own. And you will be less likely to interfere when God begins to take your child in a direction other than what you might have originally scripted for her.

## Praying for Separation

How do you pray for your child to separate well? What skills and values does she need? What lessons must he learn before he is ready to function as a healthy young adult? What should you ask God to do for her? What pinpoint prayers can you pray for your child's healthy independence? Here are a few suggestions.

### Pray that your child will trust solely in God.

In Psalm 73, the worship leader, Asaph, reflected on his relationship with God: "Whom have I in heaven but you? And earth has nothing I desire besides you. My flesh and my heart may fail, but God is the strength of my heart and my portion forever" (vv. 25–26). What a beautiful confession and prayer. Asaph admitted that the world ultimately held no allure for him. He readily acknowledged that his hope, strength, and complete dependence rested on God. Even in the loss of all his strength, Asaph knew his heavenly Father would never fail him. He also knew that his inheritance, his "portion," was in heaven.

Pray the same for your child. In these days of retirement plans, stock portfolios, and trust funds, it's easy to look to earthly things for security. If you as a parent aren't careful, you can even model a dependency on such false sources of security. When your child hits the streets as a young adult, you want him to have no doubt of where his hope and strength lie. Pray that he will know that his security and future can be found only in God. Pray that he will quickly learn the elusiveness and frailty of riches. Pray that he, like Asaph, will gladly confess that all he desires on earth is found in God.

### Pray that your child will have an unshakable character.

Knowing that their son would be raised in Pharaoh's house must have been a mixed blessing for Moses's parents. On the one hand, they knew that he would be safe, well fed, and well educated. On the other hand, they knew that he would be exposed to the false gods and licentiousness that were an everyday part of Egyptian life. Moses's folks must have prayed countless prayers for his character and integrity. Surely they prayed that he would have a heart for the one true God and that he would never succumb to the temptations that he would face in Pharaoh's house.

The writer of Hebrews tells us that God answered the prayers of Moses's parents. In Hebrews 11, where he lists numerous examples of heroic faith, the writer states that Moses "chose to be mistreated along with the people of God rather than to enjoy the pleasures of sin for a short time" (v. 25). Moses saw through the false advertising of the Egyptian paganism and rejected it in favor of obedience to the God of the Hebrews, even when that obedience meant hardship.

Pray that your child will have such noble character. Pray that she won't give in to the allure of culture or fall prey to the countless temptations that dot our Western landscape. If your child is to separate well, she will need personal integrity and wisdom to make good choices when you're not around to guide her. Pray that she will have the strength of character to stand for her God, even when pressured not to.

### Pray that your child will learn to choose delayed gratification over immediate fulfillment.

The writer of Hebrews also tells us that Moses saw the wisdom of delayed gratification. He wrote that Moses "regarded disgrace for the sake of Christ as of greater value than the treasures of Egypt, because he was looking ahead to his reward" (Heb. 11:26). We're not very good at "looking ahead" these days. We want our reward now. Everything is instant. Few of us have the discipline to make future investments or to delay benefits that might be due us. Even fewer of us are teaching such "old-fashioned" disciplines to our kids.

But Moses was on to something when he chose to delay his reward, and he was modeling more than just an old-fashioned principle when he rejected a temporal treasure for an eternal one. If our kids are to make wise choices as independent adults, then they need to know that there really is a payoff for delaying rewards. Delayed gratification is more than just holding dessert until after dinner. It's a discipline that will help our kids face the high-stakes pressures of the real world. Knowing how to say no to pleasure and yes to discomfort or inconvenience is what will help our kids learn how to save money rather than spend it, how to start a term paper on the day it's assigned rather than the week before it's due, or how to abstain from sexual behaviors until marriage.

I have a niece in college who has guys swarming her. She's a beautiful, fun, smart, and witty girl who could charm her way into the inner rings of the Pentagon if she wanted to. She's also a committed Christian. She recently agreed to go on a date with a young man to a college football game in another city. After their plans were made, some of the other girls informed her that it was customary for the girls to bring the alcohol for their dates and that she would be expected to share a bed with her date at the hotel. After my niece confirmed that those were indeed her date's expectations, she promptly broke the date. While her stand for what was right didn't go over well with some of her "popular" friends, she stood by her convictions.

How does a college freshman develop that kind of spiritual resolve? Where does a young man find the spiritual gusto to choose wisely for God; delay fun, popularity, and perks; and defer his reward to a future time? Only in knowing that being right with God is more important than being right with the world, even if it means immediate discomfort. Kids need to learn these lessons when they're young. Start praying today that your child will learn them.

Pray that your child will know that the discipline of delayed gratification is worth it. Pray that he will know that immediate payoff isn't always the best. Pray that he will have the spiritual courage to regard disgrace for the sake of Christ as of greater value than the treasures of this world. Pray that he will look ahead to his spiritual reward.

### Pray that your child will practice good financial management.

"Congratulations! Your preapproved VISA card is enclosed. Just call this number to activate your card and start spending your $5,000 line of credit." So read the notice that accompanied the shiny new credit card that was sent to my daughter, Emily—when she was thirteen! Since then, Emily has received three more "free" cards. If she had wanted to, she could now be over $20,000 in debt, and all before she graduated from high school.

A child who separates well knows the importance of good financial management. She also has a plan to support herself. You need to be involved in helping your child develop both. When she's young, give her an allowance and teach her how to save and tithe. As she gets older, help her learn how to buy wisely and not spend all her money on things she wants. As she advances in her teen years, open a checking account for her and teach her how to make and live within a budget. Even more importantly, teach her good stewardship principles. Pray that she'll learn early on the difference between owning what she has and stewarding what God has given her.

Too many kids hit young adulthood still financially dependent on their parents. They never learn to live on their own. Pray for your child to willingly and readily assume the responsibility for her own livelihood. And pray that you'll have the courage to let her.

### Pray for the courage to let your child make his own choices.

The last thing I want for my kids is failure. I'm sure you feel the same. The pain of a poor relational choice, a failed school assignment, or a blown job interview is very difficult to watch them suffer through. Beyond that, I'm just insecure enough to feel like their bad choices are somehow a reflection of my parenting skills. If I'm afraid that my kids' choices will make me look bad too, then I'm even less likely to let them fail. But let them I must, because learning to make good choices is part of their healthy separation process.

Consider how Jesus was willing to let people choose and even fail. He let the rich young ruler choose wealth over salvation. He let the Pharisees choose legalism over grace. He apparently let one of the thieves crucified with him choose hell over heaven. Jesus always made the way of truth clear to his disciples and to those who approached him. But then he let them choose. Jesus was secure enough in his relationship with his Father to let potential followers come to their own conclusions about him. He even gave his disciples enough wiggle room to fail him in his most critical time of need. In Peter's case, Jesus was able to redeem that failure and grow Peter into the stalwart leader we see in the early chapters of Acts (compare Luke 22:54–62 to Acts 2:14–41; 3:1–11; 4:8–13).

As parents, we need the wisdom to know when to intervene and rescue our kids, and when to stand back and let them fail. There are appropriate times for both. It's one thing to let your kid procrastinate in his study habits and fail a major exam; it's another to let him ride home from a party with a bunch of drunk teens. But either way, the time will come when we'll have to not only let them choose but also let them live with the consequences of their choices. Kids who are always rescued won't ever learn to take responsibility for their choices.

Solomon wrote, "A hot-tempered man must pay the penalty; if you rescue him, you will have to do it again" (Prov. 19:19). The same is true for a hot-tempered or irresponsible child: if you rescue him from the consequences of his actions, you're going to have to do it again. Pray for the wisdom and courage to let your kid fail. Pray that God will use his choices—good and bad—to develop and refine him. Pray that he will hit adulthood with the maturity to make his own choices and accept the consequences.

### Pray that your child will be relationally mature.

I remember sitting in a leadership conference where one of the speakers talked about how to recruit good leaders. Among other things, he talked about the need to pick men and women who didn't need to be "reparented." Even though I had never heard the term before, I immediately knew what the speaker was talking about. I have worked with plenty of people who needed reparenting. In fact, I'm pretty sure that I used to be one of those people.

Relationally immature people don't know how to handle themselves well in professional or social settings. They may have college or master's degrees, they may work in successful businesses, and they may look and sound like adults, but they have the relational skills of a preadolescent. I've seen adults throw complete tantrums in team meetings. I've seen workers function in a completely self-centered fashion, as if they were the only person in their work environment. I know adults who are relationally challenged. They're judgmental and gossipy, and they have such high relational barriers that it's very unlikely anyone will be able to get to know them intimately, or even want to.

Relationally challenged adults were typically coddled as children, rarely disciplined, and never taught how to cooperate with others. They hit adulthood thinking that the world revolved around them, and they typically expect their relational world to do the same.

Pray for your kid to know better. Teach your child always to value another person, regardless of social, educational, or racial differences. Pray that she'll learn to serve others and to seek the benefit of the people around her, not just her own. Pray that she will know how to handle conflict and how to cooperate and interact well with her peers. Pray that she will get her parenting needs met while she's still at home with you and not require a future spouse, employer, or roommate to finish the job you didn't.

## A Verse to Pray for Your Child

Genesis 2:24: *Father, I pray that my child will leave home well and will be dependent on you.*

# 12

## PRAYING FOR YOUR CHILD'S SPIRITUAL INHERITANCE

I T'S A GOOD thing she looks like her mother!"

I was, of course, joking. Well, sort of. My good friend and his beautiful bride had given birth to a lovely baby girl. The resemblance between mother and daughter, even at the baby's young age, was striking. They shared the same dark brown eyes. They had the same high, proud cheekbones. The baby's tiny hands and feet even looked like her mother's. I took another look at her dad and then said to the little girl, "Yep, it's a good thing your mother's genes won out."

I know you've made similar comments. I don't mean that you've poked fun at a friend the way I did. I mean you have probably commented on the recognizable traits of parents in their children. "She's got her mother's beautiful smile." "He's got his father's athletic frame." "She looks just like her mother did at that age." "He's a chip off the old block." And you know where those traits came from—our genes. Children look like their moms and dads because they get an equal number of genes from each parent. You might have your mother's smile and your father's eyes. Or you might have your father's chin and your mother's nose. We look like our parents because our DNA was basically built out of theirs.

You also probably know that we inherit more than just our physical traits from our parents. We can also inherit tendencies, behavioral patterns, and even physical weaknesses from our folks. For instance, I have really bad knees, and I've had two operations on each one. I get my bad knees from my dad. I also have arthritis in my knees and hips. Chances are I picked that up from my mom's side of the family. You could list similar health or emotional deficiencies that you inherited from your parents.

There is another type of inheritance that has eternal implications: a spiritual inheritance. What is true physically, psychologically, and emotionally is also true spiritually: we inherit many of our spiritual tendencies from our parents. It's a spiritual concept known as *generational momentum*. Simply stated, generational momentum is the spiritual direction, good or bad, that parents establish for their children. Sometimes generational momentum can be handed down for several generations, which can make it even more difficult for subsequent generations to change.

Moses learned all about generational momentum during one of his forty-day visits with God on Mount Sinai:

> Then the LORD came down in the cloud and stood there with him and proclaimed his name, the LORD. And he passed in front of Moses, proclaiming, "The LORD, the LORD, the compassionate and gracious God, slow to anger, abounding in love and faithfulness, maintaining love to thousands, and forgiving wickedness, rebellion and sin. Yet he does not leave the guilty unpunished; he punishes the children and their

children for the sin of the fathers to the third and fourth generation."

Exodus 34:5–7

Stated more directly, what we sow, others—specifically, our children—will reap.

I know it doesn't seem fair on the surface that God would punish children and grandchildren for the sins of their parents and grandparents. But I believe that God was revealing to Moses an eternal truth about sin: it always affects more than those directly involved in it. Sin's implications are far-reaching, devastating multiple lives.

As you respond to God and make choices to obey or disobey him, you send waves of spiritual implications not just to those around you but also to those who will come after you. Our spiritual choices create a tsunami of spiritual blessing or cursing that our children and grandchildren will inherit. And just like weak knees, emotional instabilities, or addictive behaviors, our spiritual weaknesses (or strengths) can quickly become even more powerful in our children's lives. When praying for our children, we need to pray against the power of our own sin's momentum and pray that they will inherit spiritual favor and blessing from us.

**Turning the Tide**

*Momentum* is "strength or force gained by motion or through the development of events."[1] You know about momentum. You've seen it in sporting events, the stock market, church growth, downhill skiing, and even relationships. Once momentum gets behind something, it can be difficult to stop.

My daughter Sara and I learned this the hard way during a recent vacation in Colorado. A giant pine tree had been cut down about two hundred yards uphill from our cabin. A dozen massive pieces of the tree's trunk, some weighing over two hundred pounds and measuring at least four feet in diameter, were left on the side of the road. Sara and I decided we needed a couple of the pieces for our cabin. We figured they'd make beautiful porch decorations and provide enough firewood for at least a dozen winters. We were able to finagle one of the massive pieces into the back of our truck, but the other chunk-o-tree was simply too big. It weighed way too much for us to lift it up into the truck.

So we started thinking, *Hmm, how do you get a two-hundred-pound, perfectly round piece of tree trunk to go two hundred yards downhill to your cabin?* The idea struck us both at the same time: *You roll it!* It seemed like a good idea initially. We set the stump on its side, turned it toward our cabin, and gave it a gentle nudge. I seriously didn't think the stump would make it twenty yards. The area was filled with rocks, small boulders, and sagebrush. I figured it would roll a few yards, fall over, and stop. I was wrong, very wrong.

I think the stump set a land speed and distance record for trunk rolling. It took off, rolled right by our cabin, crashed through a series of smaller trees, and then disappeared into a gully. There were several seconds of silence, and then we heard another crash, then silence, and then more crashing farther downhill.

At some point I began to realize that this hadn't been the best of ideas. We chased after the stump, finding a debris field of trees, plants, and rocks in its path. The area looked like a small tornado had blown through.

We found our stump resting peacefully on its side, completely unscathed from its journey, four hundred yards *downhill* from our cabin. Not to be beaten by a piece of wood, Sara and I proceeded to push that two-hundred-pound stump back *uphill* to our cabin, where it sits proudly today. I used the whole adventure as a chance to teach Sara about the laws of physics and momentum.

Spiritual momentum can be even more powerful. Once it gets rolling, it is very difficult to slow down. That's why we need to pray so diligently for our children's spiritual inheritance. We want them to have wind in *their* sails because of *our* obedience. We don't want them to have to fight battles or deal with sins we should have dealt with years ago.

So how do we turn the tide? How do we seek, through prayer, the blessing and favor of God on the next generations? What do we as parents need to do today to help our kids be spiritually healthy tomorrow?

## How to Change Momentum

Meet Josiah. He was an eight-year-old kid who lived in Jerusalem. He also happened to be the new king of Judah. His twenty-four-year-old father, Amon, had been murdered, leaving young Josiah in charge of a struggling nation. His father's reign, though brief, had not been a good one. He had led the nation to worship idols and engage in the very acts that God had clearly outlawed. Josiah's grandfather Manasseh was one of the most evil and notorious kings in Judah's history. He tried to return to God near the end of his reign, but by that point the damage had been done. His legacy was one of sorcery, witchcraft, idolatry, pagan worship, and child sacrifice. Not a good résumé for a leader of the people of God. And not a good role model for young Josiah.

But Josiah had a great-grandfather who had been different. His name was Hezekiah, and he is remembered as one of the greatest kings in Judah's history. He brought revival to Judah on multiple levels. Young Josiah hadn't inherited the best spiritual momentum from his dad and granddad, but he

159

did have the stellar example of Hezekiah to learn from. At age sixteen, Josiah decided that, like his great-grandfather, he wanted to turn the tide and shift the momentum of his family and nation back to God. He led one of the greatest reform and revival efforts in Judah's history. And he gave us a great example of how to turn the generational momentum that we or our children may have inherited.

A first great step toward turning the tide of spiritual momentum is *recognition.* If you want to bring the changes to your family that will help your kids inherit blessing, then you need to be humble enough to spot and acknowledge the need for change.

For Josiah, that wasn't difficult. The Jerusalem he ruled over included the temple, which was in disarray and disrepair. Josiah ordered the priests to clean it up. As they were doing so, they discovered an old, discarded copy of Deuteronomy. The priests brought it to the king and read it to him, and that led to a major recognition moment for Josiah: "When the king heard the words of the Law, he tore his robes. He gave these orders. . . . 'Go and inquire of the LORD for me and for the remnant in Israel and Judah about what is written in this book that has been found. Great is the LORD's anger that is poured out on us because our fathers have not kept the word of the LORD; they have not acted in accordance with all that is written in this book'" (2 Chron. 34:19–21).

It didn't take much for the young king to recognize the distance that existed between God's law and his own reality. His nation was not only engaged in countless acts that were abhorrent to God, but they had also ceased to appropriately engage in the worship that he commanded, including the observance of Passover. Josiah had his wake-up call, and it didn't take long for change to follow.

What about you? Do you need a wake-up call? Are you in touch with your reality and its proximity to the favor of

God? Have you taken time to question those family patterns, behaviors, and "elephants in the room"—issues that everyone knows are there but no one is willing to talk about?

I remember sitting in a Christian counselor's office years ago, talking about my early teenage years. As I described my rebellious days and my many wild antics, I made the flippant comment that such behavior was normal for teens, even young ones. I guessed I'd always thought my actions weren't all that unusual. But I'll never forget the shock I felt when the counselor stared soberly at me and said, "Will, that's not normal." With four simple words that man of God shattered my perception of reality and showed me the truth about my teen years. I wasn't nearly as healthy or as normal as I had thought. I had manifested attitudes and behaviors that were extreme for a young kid. I had then carried many of those attitudes into my adulthood, and I wasn't even aware of it. Even though I was a committed Christian, I still had a giant tree stump rolling out of control through the middle of my life. And as a young husband and father, I realized that I had better do something about it.

Look at your family, including the generations before you. What do you see? Do you see godliness and a spiritual heritage of faith? Or have you inherited a less-than-godly family pattern? Don't be afraid to be honest about what you see. If things aren't up to spiritual par, pray for a Josiah moment: "When the king heard the words of the Law, he tore his robes." There may need to be some robe-tearing as you start thinking about the spiritual condition of your family. But don't panic; you're on your way to revival.

Pray Psalm 139:23–24: "Search me, O God, and know my heart; test me and know my anxious thoughts. See if there is any offensive way in me, and lead me in the way everlasting." Ask God to reveal the truth about your heart, your past, your behaviors, and your spiritual momentum. Ask for a moment of clarity and recognition. Pray that you won't be blind to any hidden sinful ways that may exist in your life. Pray that, like Josiah, God will use his Word to show you the distance between his will and your reality.

Another important step in the process of changing generational momentum is *repentance*. Once you have seen the reality of your spiritual status quo, you need the courage to start changing things.

Repentance is a lost art in today's culture. To *repent* simply means to turn around and head in the opposite direction. In driving, it's a U-turn. In the military, it's an about-face. In sailing, it's coming about. There are two basic steps in repenting, and Josiah modeled both perfectly.

First, Josiah led his people to *stop* doing some things:

> The king ordered Hilkiah the high priest, the priests next in rank and the doorkeepers to remove from the temple of the LORD all the articles made for Baal and Asherah and all the starry hosts. He burned them outside Jerusalem in the fields of the Kidron Valley and took the ashes to Bethel. He did away with the pagan priests appointed by the kings of Judah to burn incense on the high places of the towns of Judah and on those around Jerusalem—those who burned incense to Baal, to the sun and moon, to the constellations and to all the starry hosts.
>
> 2 Kings 23:4–5

Josiah also got rid of all the mediums and fortune-tellers, the household gods, and the idols that dotted Judah's spiritual landscape.

This was no casual repentance. This was a major housecleaning. Josiah basically declared all-out war on pagan worship and any who participated in it. It was a costly repentance for Josiah, but it was one that God honored.

What do you need to declare war on? What behaviors, relational patterns, addictions, or practices have been passed down to you from your family that you need to end today? After God has revealed them to you in prayer, ask him to give you the courage to end them. Pray that you'll hate the sin and spiritual darkness associated with them. Ask him to show you how to cut them off from your family's life. You may need to get help from Christian friends, a small group, a pastor, or even a Christian counselor. Don't be ashamed or embarrassed. The steps you are taking, although costly, are the right ones.

Second, while Josiah was leading his nation to end some bad behaviors and practices, he was also leading them to *begin* some good ones:

> The king gave this order to all the people: "Celebrate the Passover to the LORD your God, as it is written in this Book of the Covenant." Not since the days of the judges who led Israel, nor throughout the days of the kings of Israel and the kings of Judah, had any such Passover been observed. But in the eighteenth year of King Josiah, this Passover was celebrated to the LORD in Jerusalem.
>
> 2 Kings 23:21–23

Can you imagine the emotion of that first Passover celebration? Think about the joy and excitement that Josiah, the priests, and the people must have felt in the Lord's presence as they observed their first Passover together. Think of how much it pleased God. Not only had Josiah removed the sinful practices from his nation, but he had led them to begin something beautiful and holy.

Repentance always does that. It doesn't just end bad things, it begins good ones. That's what you have to look forward to the most as you turn your generation back to God. Take great joy in knowing that as you repent, you and your children are going to discover some great new adventures in Christ-following that you can enjoy together.

One of the legacies I feel called to leave with my children is a passion for missions. Through our church's missions ministry, hundreds of families have the privilege of serving together in varying levels of cross-cultural ministry. Whether it's ministering in the inner-city projects, building houses for the poor in Mexico, or working with orphans in Nicaragua, the children in our church (including my own) are learning to love missions. Every chance I get, I serve with them. I want them to see me serving the poor, praying with widows, and loving little children. Serving with my kids in mission settings is, without exception, one of the greatest joys in my life right now. I also love knowing that hundreds of children are learning to serve and displace themselves for the benefit of others—and they're learning it from their parents' godly example.

What are you doing with your kids? Do you pray with them? Do you read the Bible together? Do you attend worship events together? Do your children learn from you the beauty of serving others? Ask God to show you what you can begin today with your children. Remember, a little obedience goes a long way with God. Just begin where you can, and he'll honor that.

There's one final step Josiah took in changing his generation's momentum. It was *instruction*. After Josiah had led his nation through many dramatic and sweeping changes, he needed to teach them why those changes were necessary and how to stay on the high road in the future. So he went to work with a major instruction effort:

> Then the king called together all the elders of Judah and Jeru-
> salem. He went up to the temple of the LORD with the men of

164

Judah, the people of Jerusalem, the priests and the Levites—all the people from the least to the greatest. He read in their hearing all the words of the Book of the Covenant, which had been found in the temple of the LORD. The king stood by his pillar and renewed the covenant in the presence of the LORD —to follow the LORD and keep his commands, regulations and decrees with all his heart and all his soul, and to obey the words of the covenant written in this book. Then he had everyone in Jerusalem and Benjamin pledge themselves to it; the people of Jerusalem did this in accordance with the covenant of God, the God of their fathers.

2 Chronicles 34:29–32

Did you see what Josiah did? He taught them God's Word, and then he led them to commit themselves to it. What a great leader! Do you want to turn the tide of generational momentum in your family? If you want to send a tsunami of spiritual blessing to the generations after you, then teach them God's Word.

If your children are young, read the Bible to them at night. If they are older, engage them in discussions or studies about the Bible. Take advantage of teachable moments (graduations, sporting wins or losses, relational hurts, failed school tests, the death of someone they knew, and so on) to plant God's Word in their souls. Mark strategic seasons of their lives by giving them a new Bible or having godly adults send

A s my daughter was getting on the bus for her first day of kindergarten, I just panicked. I literally grabbed her and whispered in her ear, "May the Lord bless and keep you, may his face shine upon you and be gracious and give you peace." It was just instinct. It wasn't planned. Since then, I have said that prayer every single day to both my children. They will not leave my presence during the day or go to sleep without that prayer. It's like a security blanket for the three of us. Even this morning when the bus pulled up, they both ran over to me and said, "Prayer."

A praying mom

Scriptures to them. Most importantly, keep them in a church that teaches the Bible to them on their level.

Pray a pinpoint prayer from Deuteronomy 6:4–9 for you, your spouse, and your children: *Lord God, we acknowledge that you are the one and only God. Help our family to love you with all our heart, soul, mind, and strength. Let your Word always be on our hearts. Help us as parents to impress your Word on our children. We ask that our kids would find it easy and natural to talk about it when they're at home, when they're away from home, and as they begin and end each day. May your holy Word be ever before them.*

## A Kingdom Success Story

I met Buddy and Melody while I was a student in seminary. Susie and I immediately found that we had much in common with this endearing couple. We both were newly married with young kids, we both were ministry-bound couples, and we both intended to live on a preacher's salary. Soon we were fast friends and spent much time together.

But we also discovered that we were very different in one major way: our respective childhoods. Susie and I were both blessed with loving, caring families. While there is no such thing as a perfect home, we both grew up in good environments. Neither Buddy nor Melody knew such favor. Both had experienced horrendous childhoods. They were the unfortunate inheritors of sinful family legacies—abuse, infidelity, alcoholism, and divorce. Both Buddy and Melody were in line to take the baton of sin and shame and pass it on to their own unfortunate offspring.

But that didn't happen. Buddy and Melody each met Jesus in their early adult years, and then they met each other. They decided that the shameful legacies passed on to them by

166

their parents and grandparents had gone on too long. They determined to be the generation that turned their family back to God.

It was Buddy who first taught me about generational momentum, and it was Buddy who first showed me how it could be changed. I'll never forget the determination and conviction with which Buddy and Melody discussed their calling. They knew that they were living their lives not for themselves but for their children and grandchildren. They were determined that Satan would no longer have any authority in their family's line. They were determined to be the generation that turned the tide back to God.

Buddy and Melody got counseling to help them own up to and understand their respective troubled childhoods. Where possible and appropriate, they talked to, confronted, and then forgave those adults who had played a role in their childhood difficulties. Then they worked diligently to be the godliest, most Christ-following family they could be. They made knowing God and serving in their church more than just an afterthought for their family. They taught and showed their kids how to love and follow Jesus. Their children were able to grow up in a world completely different and 100 percent healthier than the ones their parents had grown up in. With God's grace, Buddy and Melody really had turned their family back to God.

You can too. Pray for God to show you how to be a generation changer. Pray for him to expose the sins of your fathers. Ask him to give blessing and spiritual favor not just to your family but to multiple generations after you.

If you're just getting started and the momentum seems almost impossible to change, don't quit. God will honor your obedience. Don't despise the day of small beginnings. Remember, Jesus said that the kingdom begins with faith the size of a mustard seed (see Luke 13:18–19).

167

## A Verse to Pray for Your Child

Ephesians 6:1–4: *Lord Jesus, help my child to always obey me as he would obey you, so that your will might be accomplished in him. And help me not to exasperate him as I parent, teach, and discipline him.*

# *Appendix 1*

# A MONTH'S SUPPLY
# OF PINPOINT PRAYERS
# FOR YOUR CHILD

FOLLOWING ARE THIRTY-ONE pinpoint prayers for your child. They're in four groups, one for each week of the month, with seven prayers in each group. Three extra prayers that can be prayed at your discretion are included at the end. Each group is based on Jesus's teaching in Mark 12:29–30. After being asked what the greatest commandment was, Jesus replied, "The most important one . . . is this: 'Hear, O Israel, the Lord our God, the Lord is one. Love the Lord your God with all your heart and with all your soul and with all your mind and with all your strength.'" The command specifies four areas in which God expects us to fully love him: volitionally (heart), spiritually (soul), mentally (mind), and physically (strength).

Each of the four groups can help you pray for your child's development. The first section offers seven pinpoint prayers for your child's heart, the second for your child's soul, and so on. This prayer schedule and the enclosed prayers are a great way to pray deeply and meaningfully for your child to love God in every aspect of his or her life.

In each day's entry you'll find a verse followed by a prayer written from it. I've included the verses so you can see just how easy it is to make pinpoint prayers out of the Scriptures. Try to memorize and meditate on each day's verse. As you master its concepts, you'll be able to pray it with more confidence and passion. I pray that you'll see immediate fruit in your child's life as you pray these pinpoint prayers for him or her.

### Week One: Prayers for Your Child's Heart

#### Day 1

**Verse:** "I have hidden your word in my heart that I might not sin against you" (Ps. 119:11).
**Prayer:** *Lord God, teach my child to hide your Word in her heart so that she will not sin against you.*

#### Day 2

**Verse:** "Do not let them out of your sight, keep them within your heart" (Prov. 4:21).
**Prayer:** *God, I pray that my son will never let your words of wisdom out of his sight. Help him to keep them in his heart.*

#### Day 3

**Verse:** "Trust in the LORD with all your heart and lean not on your own understanding; in all your ways acknowledge him, and he will make your paths straight" (Prov. 3:5–6).

**Prayer:** *Father, please teach my child to trust in you with all her heart and never to trust in her own wisdom or understanding. I pray that she will acknowledge you in all her ways. And, Lord, as she does, please clearly direct her paths.*

### Day 4

**Verse:** "Blessed are the pure in heart, for they will see God" (Matt. 5:8).
**Prayer:** *Lord Jesus, please give my child a pure heart so that he might see God.*

### Day 5

**Verse:** "I will give them a heart to know me, that I am the Lord. They will be my people, and I will be their God, for they will return to me with all their heart" (Jer. 24:7).
**Prayer:** *Lord God, please give my child a heart to know you, for you are the Lord. Let her be your child, and may you be her God. Help her to seek you with all her heart.*

### Day 6

**Verse:** "I desire to do your will, O my God; your law is within my heart" (Ps. 40:8).
**Prayer:** *Holy God, may your law reside within my child's heart so that he may desire to do your will.*

### Day 7

**Verse:** "My heart says of you, 'Seek his face!' Your face, Lord, I will seek" (Ps. 27:8).
**Prayer:** *Father, let my child say, "My heart says of you, 'Seek his face!' Your face, Lord, I will seek."*

## Week Two: Prayers for Your Child's Soul

### Day 1

**Verse:** "Know also that wisdom is sweet to your soul; if you find it, there is a future hope for you, and your hope will not be cut off" (Prov. 24:14).

**Prayer:** *Holy God, may wisdom be sweet to my child's soul. As he finds it, establish his future and ensure his hope.*

### Day 2

**Verse:** "O God, you are my God, earnestly I seek you; my soul thirsts for you, my body longs for you, in a dry and weary land where there is no water" (Ps. 63:1).

**Prayer:** *O God, please be my child's God. I pray that she would seek you earnestly. Let her soul hunger and thirst for you.*

### Day 3

**Verse:** "We have this hope as an anchor for the soul, firm and secure" (Heb. 6:19).

**Prayer:** *Lord Jesus, may my child's hope in you be a firm and secure anchor for his soul.*

### Day 4

**Verse:** "Then my soul will rejoice in the LORD and delight in his salvation" (Ps. 35:9).

**Prayer:** *Mighty God, let my child's soul rejoice in you and delight in the salvation you provide.*

### Day 5

**Verse:** "My soul is consumed with longing for your laws at all times" (Ps. 119:20).

**Prayer:** *Holy Father, I pray that my child's soul would be consumed with longing for your laws at all times.*

### Day 6

**Verse:** "Give ear and come to me; hear me, that your soul may live. I will make an everlasting covenant with you, my faithful love promised to David" (Isa. 55:3).
**Prayer:** *Mighty God, I pray that my child will hear you and come to you so that her soul may live. Establish your covenant of grace with her and keep your promises to her.*

### Day 7

**Verse:** "He restores my soul. He guides me in paths of righteousness for his name's sake" (Ps. 23:3).
**Prayer:** *Lord God, please restore my child's soul. Guide him in paths of righteousness for your name's sake.*

**Week Three: Prayers for Your Child's Mind**

### Day 1

**Verse:** "Get wisdom, get understanding; do not forget my words or swerve from them" (Prov. 4:5).
**Prayer:** *Lord, please make my child hungry and thirsty for wisdom and understanding. Help her never to forget your words or stray from them.*

### Day 2

**Verse:** "The mind of sinful man is death, but the mind controlled by the Spirit is life and peace" (Rom. 8:6).

**Prayer:** *Lord Jesus, I pray that my child's mind would be controlled not by sin but by your Spirit so that he might know life and peace.*

### Day 3

**Verse:** "Do not conform any longer to the pattern of this world, but be transformed by the renewing of your mind. Then you will be able to test and approve what God's will is—his good, pleasing and perfect will" (Rom. 12:2).

**Prayer:** *Holy Father, help my child not to conform any longer to the pattern of this world but to be transformed by the renewing of her mind. Equip her to be able to test and approve what your will is—your good, pleasing, and perfect will.*

### Day 4

**Verse:** "'For who has known the mind of the Lord that he may instruct him?' But we have the mind of Christ" (1 Cor. 2:16).

**Prayer:** *Holy Father, please give my child the mind of Christ.*

### Day 5

**Verse:** "Finally, brothers, whatever is true, whatever is noble, whatever is right, whatever is pure, whatever is lovely, whatever is admirable—if anything is excellent or praiseworthy— think about such things" (Phil. 4:8).

**Prayer:** *Lord Jesus, I pray that my child's mind would dwell on things that are true, noble, right, pure, lovely, admirable, excellent, and praiseworthy.*

## Day 6

**Verse:** "Jesus turned and said to Peter, 'Get behind me, Satan! You are a stumbling block to me; you do not have in mind the things of God, but the things of men'" (Matt. 16:23).

**Prayer:** *Holy God, help my child not to think on the things of men but to think on the things of God.*

## Day 7

**Verse:** "We demolish arguments and every pretension that sets itself up against the knowledge of God, and we take captive every thought to make it obedient to Christ" (2 Cor. 10:5).

**Prayer:** *Lord Jesus, I pray that my child would learn to demolish arguments and every pretension that sets itself up against his knowledge of God, and that he would take captive every thought and make it obedient to you.*

## Week Four: Prayers for Your Child's Strength

### Day 1

**Verse:** "Therefore, I urge you, brothers, in view of God's mercy, to offer your bodies as living sacrifices, holy and pleasing to God—this is your spiritual act of worship" (Rom. 12:1).

**Prayer:** *Father, I pray that my child will submit her body to you as a living sacrifice, holy and pleasing to you, as a spiritual act of worship.*

### Day 2

**Verse:** "Do not offer the parts of your body to sin, as instruments of wickedness, but rather offer yourselves to God, as those who have been brought from death to life; and offer the parts of your body to him as instruments of righteousness" (Rom. 6:13).

**Prayer:** *Lord Jesus, help my child never to offer his body to sin, as an instrument of wickedness, but rather to God, as one who has been brought from death to life. Let his body be an instrument of righteousness.*

### Day 3

**Verse:** "For if you live according to the sinful nature, you will die; but if by the Spirit you put to death the misdeeds of the body, you will live" (Rom. 8:13).

**Prayer:** *Father, help my child not to live according to her old, sinful nature but to live by your Spirit and to put to death the misdeeds of her body.*

### Day 4

**Verse:** "The body is not meant for sexual immorality, but for the Lord, and the Lord for the body" (1 Cor. 6:13).

**Prayer:** *Lord Jesus, teach my child that his body is not meant for sexual immorality but for you, and that you hold dominion over his body.*

### Day 5

**Verse:** "Do you not know that your body is a temple of the Holy Spirit, who is in you, whom you have received from God? You are not your own; you were bought at a price. Therefore honor God with your body" (1 Cor. 6:19–20).

**Prayer:** *Father, I pray that my child would know that her body is a temple of the Holy Spirit, who is in her, whom she has received from you. Remind her that she is not her own but that she was bought at a price. Help her to honor you with her body.*

### Day 6

**Verse:** "No, I beat my body and make it my slave so that after I have preached to others, I myself will not be disqualified for the prize" (1 Cor. 9:27).

**Prayer:** *Lord God, I pray that my child would discipline his body and make it his slave so that after he has witnessed to others, he himself will not be disqualified for the prize.*

### Day 7

**Verse:** "Each of you should learn to control his own body in a way that is holy and honorable" (1 Thess. 4:4).

**Prayer:** *Lord Jesus, help my child to learn to control her body in a way that is holy and honorable.*

## And Three to Grow On!

### Day 1

**Verse:** "Whether you turn to the right or to the left, your ears will hear a voice behind you, saying, 'This is the way; walk in it'" (Isa. 30:21).

**Prayer:** *Father, I ask you to guide my child's every step. As your Word says, whether he turns to the right or to the left, let him hear your voice behind him, saying, "This is the way; walk in it."*

### Day 2

**Verse:** "But seek first his kingdom and his righteousness, and all these things will be given to you as well" (Matt. 6:33).

**Prayer:** *Lord, please make my child a kingdom seeker and kingdom builder. Help her to prioritize serving and obeying you over everything else in her life. As she does, please honor* *her obedience and give her all that she needs to succeed in today's world.*

### Day 3

**Verse:** "Don't let anyone look down on you because you are young, but set an example for the believers in speech, in life, in love, in faith and in purity" (1 Tim. 4:12).

**Prayer:** *Father, may my child not feel discouraged or insignificant because he is young, but help him set an example for the believers in speech, in life, in love, in faith, and in purity.*

# *Appendix 2*

## PRAYING FOR YOUR CHILD
## THROUGHOUT THE DAY

HERE ARE TWELVE prayer prompters to help you remember to pray for your child throughout the day. They're designed to remind you to pray at the top of each hour. So, when you have a meeting at 9 a.m., when your watch beeps at 2 p.m., or when the news comes on at 6 p.m., you'll also have a built-in prompt to pray right then for your child.

These prayer prompts include scriptural references, a prayer, and a helpful hint for remembering them.

**At 1:00:** Think about the one grateful leper—the one who remembered to go back and thank Jesus for healing him. Even though Jesus healed nine others, only one had a grateful heart (see Luke 17:11–17).

**Prayer:** *Dear Father, please give my child a heart of gratitude. Help him to always be thankful for what you have done for him and to never take your goodness for granted.*

**At 2:00:** Think about two pennies. That's the amount Jesus said someone could buy five sparrows for in his day. In that economy, sparrows obviously weren't worth much. But Jesus taught that not a single sparrow ever escapes God's notice or is forgotten by him. His point: we are of infinitely greater value to him than a sparrow. He will always watch over, provide for, and protect us (see Luke 12:6–7).

**Prayer:** *Father, I know that you value all of your creation, including sparrows. I also know that you value your children much more. Because of that, I ask you to watch over my child right now. Protect, honor, and provide for her. Please keep her in your will and close to your heart.*

**At 3:00:** Think about the number three. That's how many times Peter denied Jesus in one night. Yet Jesus forgave Peter for these grievous sins and restored their relationship. Know that no matter how your child may fail Christ today, Christ will always love and forgive him (see John 13:38; 21:15–17).

**Prayer:** *Lord Jesus, I pray that my child will have the courage to stand for you today. But if he fails you, I pray that you will forgive him and restore his relationship with you.*

**At 4:00:** Think about the number four. That's the number of men who brought their sick friend to Jesus. They were desperate and determined enough to carry their friend on a stretcher to where Jesus was. When the house Jesus was in was too crowded for them to enter, they climbed up on the roof, removed some of the roofing, and then lowered their friend down right in front of Jesus (see Mark 2:1–5). You want your kid to be like any one of those four men.

**Prayer:** *Lord Jesus, give my child an evangelistic heart. Help her to faithfully and lovingly bring her unbelieving friends to you.*

**At 5:00:** Think about the five loaves the young Hebrew boy gave to the disciples when they were looking for a way to feed the multitude of five thousand men, plus women and children (see John 6:1–13). The young boy was probably very selfless or generous or full of faith, believing that Jesus could in fact multiply what he had given. You want all three characteristics to be true about your child as well.

**Prayer:** *Lord Jesus, please make my child generous. I pray that he would have a selfless spirit and that he would believe that you will greatly increase and use what he gives you.*

**At 6:00:** Think about the six water pots filled with water at the wedding Jesus attended in Cana. When the hosts ran out of wine, Jesus turned all the water in each pot into a fine wine (see John 2:1–11). This miracle probably symbolizes many things, not the least of which is Jesus's ability to take the ordinary and make it infinitely valuable. You want him to do the same for your child.

**Prayer:** *Lord Jesus, take the dry, cheap, ordinary life that sin and Satan would dictate for my child and make it a rich, priceless, miraculous testimony to your power and glory.*

**At 7:00:** Think about a seven-year-old. That's probably about the age of the young child Jesus used as an object lesson of his kingdom. When asked about what his kingdom was like, Jesus pointed to a child and basically said, "When you think, love, and believe like a seven-year-old, you'll understand my kingdom" (see Matt. 18:1–4).

**Prayer:** *Lord Jesus, thank you that you love and exalt children. I pray that my child will always have the innocence, naïveté,*

*passion, love, and faith of a little child, even as she grows older.
Keep her heart pure toward you and your kingdom.*

**At 8:00:** Think about the number eight. That's how many days old Jesus was when Mary and Joseph dedicated him to God in the temple, just as Moses's law required (see Luke 2:21–24). You want your child to be dedicated to God every day of his life.
**Prayer:** *Lord Jesus, right now I dedicate my child's life to you. I pray that you would anoint him, bless him, protect him, and use him. I pray that he would be dedicated to you every day of his life.*

**At 9:00:** Think about Goliath, who was nine feet tall. He was a massive giant, yet young David wasn't afraid of him. He faced that giant and defeated him for the glory of God (see 1 Sam. 17:1–54). You want your child to defeat the giants in her life as well.
**Prayer:** *Holy God, I pray that my child would not be afraid of the giants in her life. I ask that you give her the strength, courage, and faith in you to face the giants that oppose her and to defeat them for your glory.*

**At 10:00:** Think about the number ten. That's how many commandments God gave to Moses. God promised that as Moses and his people obeyed his law, he would honor, prosper, and protect them (see Exod. 20:1–17; 19:3–6).
**Prayer:** *Lord God, I pray that my child will have an obedient and compliant heart. Help him to always keep your Word. As he does, I ask that you would honor and protect him.*

**At 11:00:** Think about the number eleven. That's how many disciples were left after Judas left the upper room to betray Jesus (see John 13:21–30). It's also the number of disciples that Jesus appeared to after he was resurrected (see John 20:19–20). You always want your child to be numbered among Jesus's disciples.

**Prayer:** *Lord Jesus, I pray that my child will never betray or deny you. I pray that she will always be ready to be counted as one of your disciples, even when others are turning away from you.*

**At 12:00:** Think about the number twelve. That's how old Jesus was when he wanted to spend extra time in the temple. He wanted and needed to be there. He called the temple his "Father's house" (see Luke 2:41–50). You want your child to have a passion for his heavenly Father and a desire to be in his house.

**Prayer:** *Father, I ask that you give my child a love and a passion for you. I ask that you give him a zeal for you and your house. Pull his heart to you. Let him desire to be with you, worshiping you in your house.*

# NOTES

## Chapter 1 Mariah's Miracle (and Her Mother's Prayer!)

1. From a testimony provided to the author. The mother's and daughter's names have been changed to Kathleen and Mariah, respectively, out of respect for their privacy.

## Chapter 3 Big, Hairy, Audacious Prayers for Your Child

1. Will Davis Jr., *Pray Big* (Grand Rapids: Revell, 2007).

2. The Barna Update, "Most Twentysomethings Put Christianity on the Shelf Following Spiritually Active Teen Years," The Barna Group, September 11, 2006, http://www.barna.org/FlexPage.aspx?Page=BarnaUpdate&BarnaUpdateID=245.

## Chapter 5 From the Rising of the Sun

1. "Peer Influence Paramount," Statistics Canada, May 25, 2004, http://www.statcan.ca/english/freepub/11-002-XIE/2004/05/14604/14604_04.htm.

2. B. C. Miller, "The Timing of Sexual Intercourse among Adolescents: Family, Peer, and Other Antecedents," *Youth and Society* 29, no. 1 (1997): 54–83.

3. "Positive Peer Influence," http://family.jrank.org/pages/1263/Peer-Influence-Positive-Peer-Influence.html.

## Chapter 6 All Grown Up

1. Cathy Lynn Grossman, "Young Adults Aren't Sticking with Church," *USA Today*, August 6, 2007.

## Chapter 7  Pinpoint Prayers for the Man Your Son Will Become

1. Michael Benoist, "First Person: A Survivor Looks Back," *National Geographic Adventure*, September 2004, 38.

## Chapter 9  Their Place in This World

1. Elizabeth Weiss Green, "It's All About Me," *U.S. News and World Report*, March 12, 2007, 22. See also Jean Twenge's university website, http://www.psychology.sdsu.edu/new-web/facultystaff/twenge.html.

## Chapter 10  Follow Me

1. Green, "It's All About Me," 22.

## Chapter 12  Praying for Your Child's Spiritual Inheritance

1. Merriam-Webster Online, s.v. "Momentum," http://mw1.merriam-webster.com/dictionary/momentum.

**Will Davis Jr.** is the founding and senior pastor of Austin Christian Fellowship in Austin, Texas. Will and his wife, Susie, have three children.

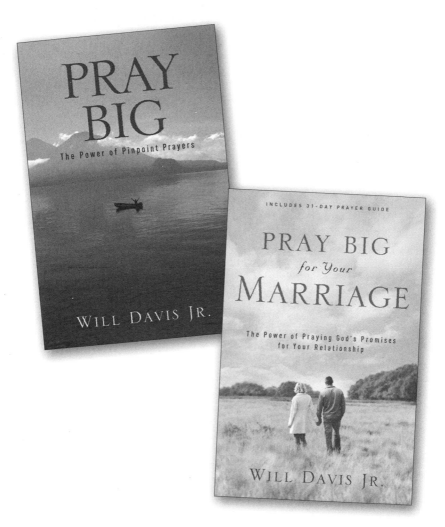

# YOU CAN BELIEVE GOD IS REAL!

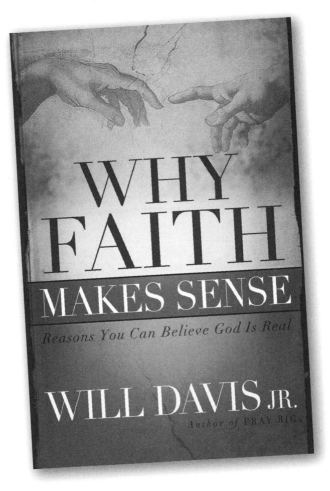

Will Davis shows lay believers and seekers that
Christianity is real, reliable, and relevant.